A Game of Failure: The 1994-95 Major League Baseball Strike

Ryan J. Eckert

ISBN: 9781549889370

Published by KDP
Seattle, WA
April 2016

INTRODUCTION

"When 25 players, a handful of coaches, and another handful of full-time front office executives can collectively generate nearly $70 million every summer, there is plenty for all. To threaten this spectacularly lucrative business by attempting to impose a dramatic change on the method of determining player salaries is a self-defeating folly."

- Roger G. Noll, August 1994

On August 12th, 1994, the Major League Baseball Players Association directed its members to go on strike, ultimately leading to cancellation of both the remainder of the 1994 baseball season and the 1994 World Series. The 232-day saga that ensued, and its fallout, would ultimately amount to the most financially and emotionally destructive episode in the history of American professional sports.

The issue predicating the strike was, according to the owners, a lack of "competitive balance," causing big market teams to have an unfair advantage in their ability to spend more than smaller market teams. Their solution was a salary cap that would theoretically eliminate the ability of teams to outspend one another. This seemed to the players to be nothing more than an attempt by ownership to reduce spending on player salaries – which averaged $1.2 million per player in 1994 – in order to increase their own profits.

The 1994 strike was not the first clash between baseball players and owners, but rather can be seen as a culmination of an extended period of labor unrest within the game throughout the second half of the twentieth century. This strike was to be the "final showdown" in the owners' long-standing efforts to break the union and forcefully impose the market control a salary cap would provide. A federal court injunction would eventually end the strike with players and owners each making concessions and resuming play in time for the (slightly delayed) 1995 season. The players emerged victorious, having succeeded in maintaining the status quo and avoiding a salary cap. The owners would get some satisfaction of their own when a "luxury tax" to share revenues among small market teams was introduced in the agreement that was made in the wake of the strike. Any victory either side could claim after the strike was over, however, was to come at an incredible price. Over $800 million in revenue was lost, and more significantly, public perception of team owners, baseball players, and the very place in American culture occupied by the sport itself would be significantly damaged.

Chapter 1 of this inquiry will examine the past history of baseball labor relations, from the earliest days of players' unsuccessful attempts to unionize, early days of player free agency, and labor schisms that led to significant work stoppages in 1972 and 1981. The late 1980s would see collusion by team owners to keep player salaries down, as well as the eventual installation of one of their own, Bud Selig, as commissioner. The effect was to set players and owners upon an unavoidable collision course.

Chapter 2 will cover the duration of the 1994-95 strike itself and the twists and turns taken by the negotiations, as well as evolving public perception. Both President Clinton and Congress issued pleas calling for the strike to end, and both were essentially ignored. As futile talks dragged on throughout the winter of 1995, owners attempted to introduce "replacement players" to break the strike, a move met with almost universal disdain.

Finally, Chapter 3 will discuss the eventual conclusion of the strike via the National Labor Relations Board and the U.S. District Court system. It will examine how the issues surrounding the strike were resolved, and how players, ownership, and fans emerged from the conflict.

The 1994-95 strike was definitive in establishing the American public's modern conception of the relationship among professional athletes, team owners, and fans. To understand how this happened, it is first useful to examine the origins of labor unrest in professional sports.

CHAPTER 1: Origins

The relationship between professional baseball players and the owners of the teams for whom they play has always been contentious. This chapter will explore the origins of struggle between these two sides, from the early days of owner dominance to the players' attempts to break free from the reserve clause that kept them bound to one team. Once players finally secured free agency, the old owner-centric economic model was compromised, leading to decades of conflict in which owners and players fought for control of exactly how baseball's new economic model would be defined.

Early Labor Conflicts

Conflicts between players and owners are rooted at the very beginnings of baseball itself, when the once-amateur game grew into a professional enterprise. Rumors of players violating the rules and receiving money under the table were circulating as early as 1860, but by 1863, the Philadelphia Athletics, soon followed by the New York and Brooklyn clubs, began openly paying players. Baseball was a business, and team owners emerged who intended to make it a profitable enterprise.[1] Owners began inserting language into contracts stipulating that players were the exclusive property of the teams that signed them, and by the 1880 season, the inclusion of such clauses became standard practice.[2] The so-called

[1] Gunther Barth, *City People: The Rise of Modern City Culture in Nineteenth-Century America* (Oxford and New York: Oxford University Press, 1980), 168-172.
[2] Peter Morris, "The Reserve Clause," *A Game of Inches: Stories Behind the Innovations that Shaped Baseball* (Chicago: Ivan R. Dee, 2010), 465.

reserve clause effectively forbade players from moving from team to team, and prevented teams from bidding against one another for players.

Naturally, players were averse to this limitation on their own earning potential and they began as early as 1885 to organize into the first players' labor union. The Brotherhood of Professional Base Ball Players, spearheaded by New York Giants star John Montgomery Ward, was unsuccessful in securing free agency and quickly moved to more drastic action, convincing some 200 players to leave and form a rival league instead.

This initial attempt to achieve bargaining solidarity was part of a larger movement toward organized labor in America at the turn of the twentieth century. Early unions like the Knights of Labor, founded in 1878, and the American Federation of Labor, founded in 1886, clashed against robber barons in a booming industrial economy. "Divided we can beg, united we can demand," read a Labor Day banner in 1886.

"Each for himself is the bosses' plea," said another slogan in 1880. "Union for all will make you free." The fledgling labor movement was gaining ground, but union leaders often found their grip on self-determination precarious. The Amalgamated Association of Iron and Steel Workers, for instance, were reminded of this fact when they were thoroughly smashed by Carnegie Steel in the Homestead Strike of 1892.[3]

The new Brotherhood League set up teams in eight cities and competed admirably against the National League's drawing power. Trade unionists suggested the Brotherhood integrate into the AFL or Knights of Labor, but the league did not immediately respond to any such offers. Instead, despite its initial promise, the Brotherhood League folded only a year after

[3] Steve Babson, *The Unfinished Struggle: Turning Points in American Labor, 1877-Present* (Lanham, MD: Rowman & Littlefield, 1999), 3-11.

its establishment, but the Brotherhood Revolt of 1890 was a sign of things to come.[4]

The first players' strike took place in 1912 when players in Detroit staged a walkout in support of their teammate Ty Cobb. After being heckled incessantly by an unruly fan at New York's Polo Grounds, Cobb jumped into the stands and assaulted the man, resulting in an indefinite suspension by the American League. His teammates refused to play their next scheduled game against Philadelphia, protesting both Cobb's suspension and baseball's lack of protection for its players. Tigers ownership was forced to field a replacement squad made up mostly of college players and team coaches, who were predictably trounced by Connie Mack's Philadelphia Athletics, 24-2.[5] The striking players, having made their point, rejoined the

[4] Paul Harper, "He Started It All: Ward Led 1890 Revolt," *Boston Globe* June 21, 1981.
[5] "Substitute Detroit Game," *New York Times*, May 9, 1912.

team the next day, and Cobb's suspension was reduced to ten games.

The players felt empowered and shortly thereafter formed a new union, the Baseball Players Fraternity. Their primary goal was to secure higher salaries, but the Fraternity was short-lived. The owners' reserve clause gave the players little leverage and negated virtually all of their bargaining power, and the Fraternity was defunct by 1917.

In 1922, baseball owners secured a major legal victory when the Supreme Court ruled in their favor in *Federal Baseball Club of Baltimore, Inc. v. National League of Prof'l Baseball Clubs*. Justice Oliver Wendell Holmes wrote, "The exhibition [of baseball], although made for money, would not be called trade or commerce in the commonly accepted use of those words. As it is put by the defendant, personal effort, not related to production, is not a subject of commerce."6 This meant that the Sherman Antitrust Act of 1890, the primary weapon of progressive trustbusters, would not apply to baseball. Owners were henceforth encouraged to continue the use of the reserve clause, as the business of baseball, including individual clubs' player contracts, could not be attacked through antitrust law. 7

These early developments in baseball labor relations would serve as lessons for each side going forward, illustrating to the players the power inherent in joining together to affect change, and the need, from the owners' perspective, to keep such a power in check. The first half of the twentieth century, however, would not see these conflicts addressed seriously. Throughout the roaring twenties, the

---

6 William B. Gould IV, "Baseball and Globalization: The Game Played and Heard and Watched 'Round the World (With Apologies to Soccer and Bobby Thomson)," *Indiana Journal of Global Legal Studies* Vol. 8, No. 1 (Fall 2000): 90.
7 Andrew Zimbalst, *May the Best Team Win: Baseball Economics and Public Policy* (Washington, DC: Brookings Institution Press, 2006), 17.

Depression, the Second World War and the postwar era, the owners were able to maintain the status quo of the reserve clause. All of this was transformed in the late 1960s and early 1970s when the Major League Baseball Players Association and its leader, Marvin Miller, demanded a change.

Marvin Miller and the MLBPA

During America's post-World War II boom, union representation became increasingly ubiquitous in society, and relations between management and labor seemed to transform from animosity into more cooperative, mutually beneficial tacit agreements. However, this existential acceptance of unions is not to be confused with labor peace; the terms of relationships between unions and owners were often determined through massive

confrontations and lengthy court battles.8 In
1954, disgruntled with lack of owner response to
their demands for an upgraded pension plan, the
players decided to form a new union of their
own, the Major League Baseball Players
Association. The MLBPA spent its early years
under its first president Bob Feller falling into
the same paternalistic, subordinate relationship
with the owners, which players' organizations
had traditionally assumed in the past. Not yet a
bargaining unit, the union could only make
demands and hope that owners would listen.
This changed when the players hired a former
executive for the Steelworkers Union, Marvin
Miller, in 1966.

By the mid-1960's, labor in America was
winning its political battles. Upon the 1964
election of President Lyndon Johnson – a
candidate strongly backed by unions – AFL-CIO

8 Nelson Lichtenstein, *State of the Union: A Century of
American Labor* (Princeton: Princeton University Press,
2003), 98-99.

leader George Meany declared, "To a greater degree than ever before in the history of this country, the stated goals of the Administration and of Congress, on one hand, and of the labor movement, on the other, are identical."[9] Unions were experiencing a fundamental change in how they viewed themselves. "Thirty years ago," a garment union leader wrote, "...Organize! Strike! Settle! That was labor-management relations." But today, he explained, "most of our problems are settled at the conference table through negotiations. This requires new skills, a different kind of intelligence. Now it is diplomacy instead of the big stick."[10] Baseball's new union leader, Marvin Miller, fit this fresh mold perfectly. Miller brought the confrontational, pressure-heavy political tactics of mainstream labor relations into the previously hermetically-sealed world of baseball labor, and the results were revolutionary.

[9] Babson, *The Unfinished Struggle*, 146-147.
[10] *Ibid.*

Miller went to work immediately, and 1968 saw the owners and the Players Association draft their first collective bargaining agreement (CBA). The new deal raised minimum salaries from $6,000 to $10,000 and established a formal grievance process. The reserve clause, a highly contentious issue for both sides, was tabled for the time being.

The changes it contained were far from radical, but the 1968 CBA was a pivotal moment in baseball's labor movement. Miller, despite his hard-nosed reputation, was able to surreptitiously change the fundamental relationship between players and owners by the mere act of entering into a process of collective bargaining. The 1968 agreement set the precedent that collectively bargained agreements, rather than owners' pronouncements, would dictate the course of owner-player relations from now on.[11] "We had

[11] Zimbalist, *May the Best Team Win*, 77-78.

put real restrictions on the power of the owners either to change rules unilaterally or ignore established ones when it suited their whims," Miller would later recall. "In other words, clubs could no longer play sheriff, judge, and jury with ballplayers."[12]

Curt Flood Case

In 1969, St. Louis center fielder Curt Flood refused to accept a trade his club had negotiated that would have sent him to Philadelphia. He instead requested to become a free agent. "Dear Mr. Kuhn," Flood wrote the Commissioner, "After twelve years in the major leagues, I do not feel that I am a piece of property to be bought and sold irrespective of my wishes."[13] His request was summarily denied, and

[12] Marvin Miller, *A Whole Different Ball Game: The Inside Story of the Baseball Revolution* (Chicago: Ivan R. Dee, 1991, 2004), 97.
[13] Neil F. Flynn, *Baseball's Reserve System: The Case and Trial of Curt Flood v. Major League Baseball* (Springfield, IL: Walnut Park Group, 2006), 2-7, 45.

Flood, arguing that his basic constitutional rights were violated by the reserve clause, took legal action. With the financial backing of the players union, Flood sued MLB in federal court. Flood lost and subsequently appealed, and the case eventually ended up in 1972 before the U.S. Supreme Court. The Supreme Court upheld the decision of the lower courts, and Flood was defeated.

The case was a failure for Curt Flood, but the consequences of *Flood v. Kuhn* were far-reaching. The court's decision had been influenced strongly by the relatively recent formation of the MLBPA. Since the players were unionized, and terms of their agreement with MLB were a product of collective bargaining, then MLB could not be held in violation of antitrust law.[14] Flood's rebuttal stated that the newly-formed union had not been given "time to

[14] Kieran M. Corcoran, "When Does the Buzzer Sound?: The Nonstatutory Labor Exemption in Professional Sports," *Columbia Law Review* Vol. 94, No. 3 (April 1994): 1045.

modify or eradicate the reserve clause system
that was thrust upon the players," but his pleas
fell on deaf ears.15

The outcome of *Flood* confirmed for both
players and owners that MLB's antitrust
exemption was virtually invulnerable. Future
conflicts between the two sides would thereby
not be successfully resolved by litigation, but
through collective bargaining. Going forward,
the players, steadfast in their desire to eliminate
or at least modify the reserve clause, would
commit to an increasingly aggressive bargaining
posture as a result, with Marvin Miller at the
helm.

1972 Strike and late 70's

The new collective bargaining agreement
in 1970 enacted the first modifications to the
reserve clause in nearly a century. The "five and

---

15 Gould, "Baseball and Globalization," 96.

ten" rule went into effect, allowing a player with ten years of service in MLB and five with his current club the right to waive any trade to another team. Curt Flood, having played for St. Louis for more than ten years, would have been protected by this rule when his team attempted to trade him to Philadelphia. Alas, Flood's case had already been lost in district court and was making its way through the circuit of appeals by the time the new rule went into effect.

More significantly, the 1970 agreement ratified a provision proposed for third-party arbitration. Previously, the 1968 agreement had established a grievance procedure, with the Commissioner serving as final arbiter. Now teams and players, if unable to reach terms of a dispute on their own, could go before a third party arbitrator who would make a final, binding decision. The looming threat of binding arbitration would, in theory, make it easier for both sides to reach compromises without resorting to arbitration at all. [16]

Arbitration was designed to engender a new spirit of cooperation, but friction between players and owners remained. As spring training began in 1972, the players wanted the owners to disburse a surplus that had accumulated in their pension fund, but the owners refused. Expecting to stare down the players with ease, the owners were instead shocked when the MLBPA initiated their first strike. The players' walkout took place over the last five days of spring training and the first nine days of the 1972 season, cancelling a total of 86 regular-season games. [17] The owners quickly capitulated and increased contributions to player pensions. The issue at hand was relatively trivial, but the 1972 strike was an even greater moral victory for the players union, effectively demonstrating their solidarity and flexing their power. Owners underestimated

[16] Gould, "Baseball and Globalization," 97.
[17] Zimbalist, *May the Best Team Win*, 78-80.

player resolve, a mistake they would go on to make several more times in the coming decades.18

The provision for third-party arbitration, which originated in 1970, was expanded slightly in 1973. As fate would have it, the arbitration process proved to be the means by which the reserve clause was successfully challenged and ultimately defeated. The first arbitration case was a 1974 dispute between Jim "Catfish" Hunter and Oakland owner Charles Finley. Arbitrator Peter Seitz ruled that Finley violated the terms of Hunter's contract by failing to make an agreed-upon contribution toward his annuity, thus rendering the contract null and void. Due to Seitz's ruling, Hunter became baseball's first free agent via technicality.19 After fielding multi-million dollar bids from the Mets, Cardinals,

18 William B. Gould IV, *Bargaining with Baseball: Labor Relations in an Age of Prosperous Turmoil* (Jefferson, NC: McFarland and Co., 2011), 76-78.
19 Flynn, *Baseball's Reserve System*, 316.

Twins, Angels, Indians, Braves, Phillies, Pirates, Red Sox and Royals, Hunter settled on the Yankees, accepting their offer of $3.5 million with a $1 million signing bonus.[20] The entire baseball world took notice, and Hunter's massive new contract illustrated just how high the stakes of free agency were for both players and owners alike.

In 1975, Seitz once again sided with the players in a grievance filed by pitchers Dave McNally of the Expos and Andy Messersmith of the Dodgers. Both players lobbied for free agent status after completing the terms of their contracts. Like virtually all "standard" player contracts at the time, their contracts were five-year deals with a final one-year club option that could be invoked after the contract ended. Since 1880, the standing interpretation of the reserve clause allowed clubs to exercise this one-year renewal option in perpetuity. McNally and

[20] John Heylar, *Lords of the Realm: The Real History of Baseball* (New York: Ballantine, 1994), 152-157.

Messersmith rejected that interpretation, and Seitz agreed. In his decision, Seitz stated that once a player completed the terms of his contract for the specified number of years it contained, the contract was fulfilled, and he was thus a free agent. The single year club option, he ruled, could only be initiated once unless specified otherwise.

The owners' immediate response was to fire Seitz from his position as arbitrator. Despite the owners' efforts to have the ruling overturned, the Eighth Circuit Court of Appeals upheld the decision, and the owners were left with no recourse.[21] Seitz, in his decision, effectively abolished the reserve clause that kept players bound to one club for nearly a century. This decisive ruling ushered in a new era of free agency in baseball.

[21] Jim Kaplan, "No Games Today," *Sports Illustrated* June 22, 1981: 18.

The Seitz decision effectively meant that all the players whose contracts expired at the end of 1976 would become free agents. The MLBPA realized that flooding the market with talent in such a way would have a less positive effect on player salaries overall, so they agreed to a four-year agreement that would limit the free-agent option to players with six years of experience.22 By 1980, the four-year agreement of 1976 was due to expire. The owners, anticipating a looming conflict, took preventative measures and hastily funded a strike war chest of over $15 million. Additionally, a new chief negotiator was brought in to head the Player Relations Committee. Ray Grebey, like his counterpart Miller, came from the mainstream labor world, having worked previously as chief corporate negotiator for General Electric. Grebey was brought into match the bellicose tactics of Miller, and he embraced his role as union-buster

22 *Ibid.*, 19.

with zeal.23 When the expiration of the
agreement arrived, the players predictably
expressed their desire for the new agreement to
reduce the eligibility period for salary arbitration
as well as reduce limits on free agency, but the
owners were determined to give no further
concessions. Furthermore, the owners sought to
curb rising player salaries due to free agency by
installing provisions to keep the free-agent
market in check. They proposed that a team that
signed a free agent would have to somehow
compensate the player's former team,
discouraging teams to sign recklessly lest they
lose a valuable player of their own. Neither side
could agree on the specifics for such a
compensation plan.

Negotiations were deadlocked heading
into 1980, and the players, hoping to force the
owners' hand, went on strike for the final eight
days of spring training. After the cancellation of

23 Zimbalist, *May the Best Team Win*, 80-81.

92 exhibition games, cooler heads prevailed, and a strike affecting the 1980 regular season was averted. The expansion of free agency was the only issue on which both sides could not manage to agree. Players and owners drafted a new four-year agreement, each consenting to establish a joint study committee and put off the issue of free agency until the following year.[24] The result, when the committee unsurprisingly came back empty handed, would be the first mid-season work stoppage in baseball history.

1981 Strike

Tensions were high coming into the 1981 season, with the question of free agency still unresolved as spring training broke. The owners suggested that since no negotiated agreement could be reached, they were simply going to put their own free agency plan into effect. The

[24] Paul D. Staudohar, "The Baseball Strike of 1994-95," *Monthly Labor Review* March 1997: 21-22.

players declared a strike in response, beginning
on June 12, 1981. The Federal Mediation and
Conciliation Service was brought in to help, but
was ultimately unsuccessful due to its lack of any
binding arbitrative authority. 25 Another factor
that may have prolonged the 1981 strike was the
contentious relationship between the lead
negotiators for both sides. Marvin Miller and his
negotiating opponent, Ray Grebey, were unable
to work together harmoniously due to stark
differences in personality and Miller's
willingness to publicly criticize Grebey in the
media. As the strike continued, Miller withdrew
himself from the bargaining table amid owners'
accusations of obstructing a settlement. MLBPA
council Donald Fehr, Miller's heir apparent, took
his place as chief negotiator. Fifty days and 712
cancelled games later, with the owners' reserve
fund almost depleted, the two sides struck a deal.
A free-agent compensation model was agreed

25 Kaplan, "No Games Today," 19.

upon, the specifics of which were determined through a rather complex formula that lacked the teeth owners originally envisioned. Indeed, the compensation plan did little to curb rising player salaries, and both sides were left having achieved little progress after 1981. Losses, however, were significant, resulting in over $72 million in lost revenue for the owners and $34 million in salaries sacrificed by the players.[26] The 1981 strike was, from the owners' perspective, a very expensive exercise in futility.

Baseball was set to return in August, beginning with the All-Star Game on August 9th. The owners devised a perplexing scheduling arrangement for the resumption of play whereby division winners in each half of the strike-split season played in a one-game playoff at the season's end. Fan reactions were mixed. Average attendance in the first half of 1981 dropped 11%

[26] Zimbalist, *May the Best Team Win*, 81.

after the season resumed.27   A *Sports Illustrated* article written in the midst of the strike cited a poll in which 53% of fans sided with the owners, although it was left unclear how many of the remaining 47% supported players, sided with neither party, or remained undecided. The article's title, "Strike! The Walkout the Owners Provoked," certainly made the magazine's position clear. "The owners may not have wanted a strike," wrote author Jim Kaplan, "but they had their reasons to provoke it." He continued, "Some owners melodramatically cast the strike as the ultimate showdown with Miller (who is expected to retire this year) for 'control of the game.' So they pushed the players to the brink – and beyond."28

The summer of 1981 also saw another high-profile labor dispute play out in the public eye between President Ronald Reagan and

27 Lee Lowenfish, *The Imperfect Diamond: A History of Baseball's Labor Wars* (Lincoln, NE: University of Nebraska Press, 2010), 246.
28 Kaplan, "No Games Today," 19.

federal employees of the Professional Air Traffic Controllers Association (PATCO). PATCO members felt they were chronically overworked and understaffed, but were unable to muster public support for a strike. Instead, the common perception was that of a white-collar union willing to disrupt national air travel by striking for higher wages, which already nearly doubled the national median. President Ronald Reagan, himself a former union president, ordered the firing of 11,300 PATCO members after three days on strike, a decision supported by nearly 60% of the American public. [29]   This marked a turning point in the American labor movement and the beginning of a downward slide in labor's power and prestige. The lesson learned by management was that by provoking a strike, owners could induce unions to use their own ultimate weapon fatally against themselves. In the wake of the PATCO strike, writes author

[29] Babson, *The Unfinished Struggle*, 155-157.

Joseph A. McCartin, "prominent employers saw strikes not as conflicts to be avoided, but as opportunities to break or tame unions."[30]

Although baseball's owners were badly defeated after the 1981 strike, this momentous victory by management over labor, as well as the shift in national labor climate it indicated, must have provided the owners some degree of encouragement. The owners did not abandon their desire to break the players union. It would be thirteen years, however, before they would get another chance at the "ultimate showdown" they sought.

Collision Course to 1994

In 1985, players and owners signed a new five-year agreement, the centerpiece of which

---

[30] Joseph A. McCartin, *Collision Course: Ronald Reagan, The Air Traffic Controllers, and the Strike that Changed America* (New York: Oxford University Press, 2011), 348.

was a new method of salary arbitration. The players bristled and went on strike, but the man who replaced Kuhn in 1984, new commissioner Peter Uberroth, was able to bring the action to a resolution after just two days. [31] Players received a minimum salary increase from $40,000 to $60,000 and an increased contribution to their pension fund; in exchange, they agreed to increase the service requirement for salary arbitration from two to three years.[32] Uberroth had managed to "save baseball" and annoy his new employers in the process, leaving out of the agreement many of the conditions the owners hoped to achieve and then announcing the agreement before the owners approved it. Uberroth's response to his critics was to present a new method for owners to keep player salaries from escalating – not by aggressive collective bargaining, but by simply colluding behind the scenes. At owner meetings Uberroth organized,

[31] Staudohar, "The Baseball Strike of 1994-95," 23.
[32] Zimbalist, *May the Best Team Win*, 82.

he imprudently reminded owners that it was perfectly legal to casually discuss not signing free agents, as long as they avoided making any formal agreements not to sign them.[33]

It did not take long for players to note the drastically reduced free-agent market and sense that something foul was afoot, and in 1986 the MLBPA filed the first of several grievances. The collusion of 1986-1988 would lead to settlements costing the owners a total of $280 million in damages. More significantly, it would fill the players with distrust for owners that would poison relations between the two for years to come.[34] "The owners' disgraceful regard for their written contractual commitment... resulted in a shift of at least a third of a billion dollars out of players' salaries into the owners' coffers, and prematurely ended the careers of a number of players," Marvin Miller wrote in 1991.

[33] Andrew Zimbalist, *In the Best Interests of Baseball?: The Revolutionary Reign of Bud Selig* (Hoboken: John Wiley & Sons, 2006), 90-94.
[34] Zimbalist, *May the Best Team Win*, 84-85.

"George Steinbrenner and Ted Turner and the burger and beer barons who run major league baseball love to... tell America's young idealists about the glories of the free enterprise system, but the truth is that they have spent the better part of their entire baseball lives trying to avoid it."[35] Any player naïve enough to believe in the spirit of cooperation before the collusion episode was surely now convinced otherwise.

Uberroth's successor, Bart Giamatti, died after only five months in office, a short tenure in which he managed to leave his mark on the game by issuing a permanent suspension to Pete Rose. A search committee headed by Milwaukee owner Bud Selig quickly appointed a replacement, Giamatti's friend and former Deputy Commissioner Fay Vincent. Vincent's initial test after taking office was an earthquake that struck before game three of the 1989 World Series in

---

[35] Miller, *A Whole Different Ball Game*, 351-352.

Oakland; it was the first of many disasters that would mark his tenure as commissioner. 36

When the next CBA expired in 1990, owners decided to seek several drastic changes and attempted to force the issue with a spring training lockout. The lockout ensued for 32 days but ended suddenly when Fay Vincent, invoking his power to act "in the best interests of baseball," ordered training camp to reopen. Vincent's declaration terminated the lockout abruptly, spoiled the owners' efforts, and ingratiated him to none of them.37 Vincent made public statements with his own recommendations for a new agreement, many of which supported the players and the status quo, and served to make the owners' proposals seem even more radical by contrast. Consequently, these proposals – which included a salary cap to limit total expenditures on player salaries for each team as well as a pay-for-performance

36 Zimbalist, *In the Best Interests of Baseball?*, 99-103
37 *Ibid.*, 100-110.

compensation scheme in which players with less than six years of major league playing time would have their salaries computed by statistical formulas – were left on the table.[38]

The owners, feeling scorned by Vincent and still unsatisfied, began to set into motion the events that would lead directly to the 1994-95 strike. Their first move was a coup to unseat Fay Vincent as commissioner. A movement grew within the ranks of ownership to remove Vincent, spearheaded by Chicago White Sox owner Jerry Reinsdorf and Milwaukee owner Bud Selig. However, the legal grounds on which they could do so were initially unclear. The charter of Major League Baseball stated, as written by renowned early Commissioner Kenesaw Mountain Landis, that "no diminution of the compensation or power of the present or any succeeding Commissioner shall be made during his term of office." In other words,

---

[38] Staudohar, "The Baseball Strike of 1994-95," 23.

Vincent couldn't be fired outright, or so it seemed. In the past, when a commissioner ran afoul of ownership, the owners simply gave him the cold shoulder and expressed, informally, their lack of confidence. Most of the time, as was the case with Bowie Kuhn, the commissioner got the hint sooner or later and stepped down. Vincent, though, when presented with growing dissatisfaction among the owners, took a defiant stance, and proclaimed that he could not be forced out nor would he resign under any circumstances. The owners felt they gave Vincent a chance to leave quietly and save face, but his public challenge only strengthened their resolve to force him out. The owners gathered together and took a vote, and with a two-thirds majority of 18-9 with one abstention, they agreed to publicly issue a resolution of no confidence. Vincent, previously defiant, was emotionally crushed and tendered his resignation.[39] Bud Selig became "acting commissioner" in 1992 and would hold that temporary title until his official appointment in 1998. In the meantime, there was work to do.

The owners would no longer bother to maintain the fiction that the commissioner was an independent power, as the likes of Mountain Landis had actually been. Bolstered by their success in Vincent's ouster, the owners voted to reopen negotiations on salaries and free agency in December 1992. Throughout 1993, a few meetings took place between the owners and the union, but no real offers were made. By December 1993, the previous four-year CBA expired and the owners voted unanimously to share revenue and pursue a salary cap for the players.

The owners supported a two-pronged approach of a salary cap and revenue sharing as a solution to the supposed problem of

[39] Heylar, *Lords of the Realm*, 540-551.

competitive balance. They argued that big-market teams were outspending – and thereby unfairly dominating – the small-market teams. The solution was to limit player salaries to curb teams from outspending one another, but a salary cap alone would leave another problem. Under the old model, the big-market teams were generating more revenue than the small market teams due to their market size, and were reinvesting it back into free-agent acquisitions, thus creating, as the owners claimed, a lack of competitive balance. With a salary cap, those teams, now prevented from reinvesting their profits into players, would become much more profitable than their small-market colleagues. Consequently, the small and mid-market teams desired revenue sharing, or the creation of a mutual funding pool to offset baseball expenses that would otherwise threaten their clubs' profitability.

Another major factor precipitating the crisis was the revision of MLB's national television contracts in 1993. Generally, MLB teams receive a significant portion of their revenue from both local and national television broadcast contracts. While Individual teams negotiate and receive revenue from their own local television contracts, teams divide revenue from national broadcast contracts equally among each club. Accordingly, as the 1994-95 strike loomed, small-market teams with meager local broadcast markets were much more dependent on revenue from national broadcast contracts than were their big-market equivalents, as there was a significant amount of money involved; national contracts with NBC and ABC from 1984 through 1989 generated $1.125 billion.

Beginning in 1990, MLB inked new four-year television deals with CBS and ESPN, which were economic flops for both networks. CBS, hoping to gain prestige by expanding its sports programming, paid $1.1 billion for a broadcast rights package including the playoffs and World Series but received only twelve regular season games, compared to the forty regular-season games shown by NBC and ABC for roughly the same amount. The ESPN contract was made for 175 regular-season games, but the up-and-coming cable network was still unavailable in about half of American homes. Fans were frustrated with the lack of coverage, and both networks lost money on the deal – about $150 million for ESPN and $500 million for CBS.[40]

When the CBS contract expired, networks approached negotiations more cautiously as they dramatically restructured the terms of their broadcast agreements. A new arrangement was initiated in 1993 in the form of a joint venture among ABC, NBC and MLB called The Baseball Network. The networks offered MLB no up-front money, but instead conceded the rights to sell advertising time during broadcasts and subsequently keep between 80 and 85 percent of

[40] Paul D. Staudohar, *Playing for Dollars: Labor Relations and the Sports Business* (Ithaca and London: Cornell University Press, 1996), 19-22.

revenue from airtime sold. A separate contract with ESPN for weekday games was signed for $225 million for six years, down from the previous contract of $400 million for four years.41 As a result of these restructured television deals, national broadcast revenues were cut by as much as 50% from previous years, creating substantial financial anxiety which underscored owners' yearnings for change to the CBA in 1993.

The proposals of 1993 represented the most radical redrawing of the status quo since free agency began in 1975. Ever since the Messersmith-McNally decision, the owners' attempts to rein in the union and stop player salaries from spiraling upwards were ineffective. Now, the owners felt, was the time to dig in their heels, subdue the union, and force a radical market intervention. The stage was set for the ultimate showdown for control of the game.

41 *Ibid.*

CHAPTER 2: Strike

Since the advent of free agency in 1975, many owners struggled to accept baseball's new economic model. Owners bemoaned an increasingly powerful players union and fought in vain to keep rising salaries in check. Their restlessness with the new status quo grew until the 1990s, when owners voted to oust Commissioner Fay Vincent and install one of their own, Bud Selig, into the Commissioner's office. The obstacles preventing them from all-out war with the players union in the past were gone, and in 1992 they voted to reopen the collective bargaining agreement. It was time, the owners believed, to finally take back control of the game.

Before the Strike: Competitive Balance?

The owners maintained that the decision to aggressively push for a salary cap and free agency was predicated on a lack of "competitive balance" in baseball. Their position was that wildly escalating player salaries left small-market teams unable to keep up with big-market teams' spending, allowing the big-market teams to unfairly dominate the game on the field. The players denied these claims, and had some compelling evidence on their side.

In the fifteen years preceding the strike, baseball clearly did have competitive parity: of the 26 major league teams (excluding the two expansion teams added in Colorado and Florida in 1993), 23 different teams won division titles, 18 of those won league championships, and 12 won a World Series. The Yankees and Mets in New York, the biggest market of them all, won only two pennants between them. At the time of the strike, four of the bottom six teams by revenue – Cleveland, Houston, Montreal and Seattle – were legitimate contenders, either in first place or within two games of first place. The Toronto Blue Jays, with a payroll of $55 million that exceeded the total revenue of all six of the bottom teams, were sixteen games out in the AL East.[42]

The owners continually pointed out that the average players' salary in 1994 was $1.2 million, but this, too, was misleading. That average figure was skewed by outliers like the Mets' Bobby Bonilla, the game's highest paid player in 1994 at $6.3 million, Chicago's Ryne Sandberg ($5.9 million), and Toronto's Joe Carter ($5.5 million).[43] In fact, the top 12% of the players made up 54% of major league payrolls in 1994. From the players' perspective, it was median salary, about $450,000 per player that

42 Jack McCallum, "Blame the Bosses," *Sports Illustrated* October 10, 1994.
43 Alan Schwarz, "'94 in Review," *Baseball America 1995 Almanac*, ed. Allan Simpson (Durham, NC: Baseball America, 1995), 9.

year, which more accurately represented how much a typical major leaguer made.44

Furthermore, the outlandishly large contracts that drove up team payrolls were, the players argued, a product of the owner's own reckless spending. Any team that wanted to curb their imprudent spending and impose a *de facto* salary cap on their own payroll was already free to do so at any time, as the struggling Mariners did in 1994 by limiting their GM to a budget of $29 million. Besides, since the owners bought their teams as investments with the hopes that the forces of the free market would increase their value over time, they had no right to refuse to let the same free market forces set the value of players' salaries.45

The MLBPA also called into question the notion that the game as a whole was losing

44 Paul D. Staudohar, "Baseball's Changing Salary Structure," *Compensation and Working Conditions* Fall 1997, 5-7.
45 Jack McCallum, "Blame the Bosses," *Sports Illustrated* October 10, 1994.

money. The owners alleged that as many as nineteen teams were on pace to lose money in 1994, and made their financial statements from 1991-1993 available to the players to substantiate their assertions. The union commissioned Stanford economist Roger G. Noll to analyze and interpret the data, and Noll's report refuted almost all of the owners claims. "Baseball is financially healthy," he writes. "In each year, a few teams actually do lose money... but no teams, not even those in the smallest markets, are fated to be persistent losers in the present structure." The claim that nineteen teams will lose money, the report held, was completely without merit.

Noll also repudiated the idea that the supposed need for financial restructuring was linked to a projected decline in national broadcast revenues. The value of the broadcast contracts were hurt, he admits, by the recession that was underway when they were negotiated, as well as by competition from cable television that was making national networks less profitable. "Nevertheless," Noll asserts, "the most recent national broadcasting contracts were worse for baseball than they should have been, reflecting poor business judgment on the part of management about the long-run attractiveness of their product to national broadcasters." In other words, the owners were not the victims of market factors that lowered their national broadcast revenue, but they had simply used bad judgment and signed a bad contract, for whom they had no one to blame but themselves.[46]

Furthermore, despite what the owners said, player salaries were not increasing faster than revenues, and thus, salaries could not be held to be the cause of the owners' financial problems. The real cause of the declining finances of baseball is obvious to Noll: the

[46] Roger G. Noll, "Baseball Economics in the 1990s: A Report to the Major League Baseball Players Association (Public Version)," BHOF Central Archives: MFF3, 1994: 1-36.

inherent inability of the current system to facilitate action among the owners. He writes,

> Baseball's problems stem from its operating rules – the requirement that almost any significant action receive supermajority support. Because teams have many natural conflicts of interest, and compete against each other both artistically and economically, supermajorities are almost impossible to bring together. Hence, baseball cannot deal coherently with broadcasting (and has not for fifty years), cannot agree how rapidly to expand and where to put the teams, cannot define the job of commissioner let alone hire one, and cannot even adopt division alignments and playing schedules that would both increase fan interest and reduce costs. But baseball owners can agree about their uniform interest in reducing player salaries and obtaining more concessions from government; hence perpetual confrontations with players in the quest for give-backs and with federal, state and local political leaders for stadium subsidies, tax breaks, and antitrust exemptions.[47]

[47] Noll, "Baseball Economics in the 1990s," 36 .

Roger G. Noll's report did a great deal to inform players' attitudes as negotiations with the owners took place throughout the summer of 1994. As far as the union was concerned, the owners were unable to get their financial house in order and wanted the players to pay the price; attacking player salaries wasn't the most constructive solution, but rather the only thing on which all the owners could actually agree. The players expected the owners to make excessive demands. What the owners actually did propose, however, was even more radical and far-reaching than the players ever anticipated.

The Owners' Proposal

The owners met at their yearly winter meetings in December 1992 and voted to reopen the collective bargaining agreement with the players. The current agreement, signed in the wake of the 1990 lockout, was a four-year deal not set to expire until January 1994, but each side had the option of reopening after the agreement's third year. The decision to reopen the agreement was bolstered by a coinciding change in the owners' own voting rules: previously, a simple majority was needed to initiate a lockout, but this requirement was changed to a three-fourths majority. This helped convince hesitant owners of profitable teams that reopening the agreement could result in a more beneficial business model without necessarily causing a work stoppage, as it had in 1990. Even with this reassurance, only 15 clubs voted to reopen with 13 voting against, but the majority won the day. The owners' tone, however, was peaceful: "We are not seeking a confrontation," Richard Ravitch, the owners' chief negotiator told the media. "We would like to move for some changes in the players' compensation system." The owners assured that the current agreement would be honored through the end of the 1993 season, while the specifics of those "changes" were determined.[48]

Throughout 1993 the Player Relations Committee (PRC), the owners' bargaining arm, met sporadically with union representatives, but neither side made any tangible offers nor demonstrated any real sense of urgency. Finally, on June 14, 1994, almost eighteen months after voting to reopen the agreement, the owners unveiled their proposal for a new contract.

Their proposition contained several drastic, fundamental changes. They proposed a 7-year deal in which owners and players would split revenues 50-50. The proposal eliminated salary arbitration, but in exchange allowed players with four years of major league service to become free agents, compared with the previous six year requirement. However, any free agent's current club would have the right to

[48] Jerome Holtzman, "Owners Reopen Basic Agreement, but Lockout Unlikely in '93," *Chicago Tribune* December 8, 1992.

match any offer the player might receive on the open market for players with less than six years of service. Players with less than four years of service would be paid based on an escalating scale of minimum salaries, which were to be determined later by collective bargaining. The 50-50 split the owners proposed applied to all revenue streams, including licensing revenue from lucrative merchandising deals. Players' health insurance, pension contributions, and benefits, previously paid by their employers, would now come out of the players' 50% share. Most significantly, the owners wanted a salary cap. They sought a cap that would be phased in over the next 4 years, restricting club payrolls to no more than 110% of the league average, with a minimum salary "floor" of 84%.[49]

The players objected for several reasons. The owners' proposed 50-50 split of profits would be a step backwards from the share the

[49] Staudohar, "The Baseball Strike of 1994-95," 25.

players were currently receiving – between 3%
and 6%.50 They certainly did not wish to give
away half of the licensing revenue they were
making by selling their own likenesses to
companies producing baseball cards, video
games, and memorabilia. This licensing money
amounted to over $50 million per year and was
used as the primary funding source for their
strike fund. Likewise, they objected to their
substantial benefits packages coming out of their
share of revenues. In fact, the union argued that
after including these new expenses, which were
previously paid for by the owners, the share of
revenues they would be left with would be closer
to 40%.51 Union counsel Gene Orza summed up
the players' reaction: "How could the owners
believe this is the kind of proposal we could be

---

50 Zimbalist, *In the Best Interests of Baseball?,* 146-147.
51 Murray Chass, "Baseball: Under Proposal, Players Could
Get Lesser Share," *New York Times* June 18, 1994: 1.31.

happy with? The revenue they're sharing is the players' revenue."[52]

The loss of salary arbitration was seen as another step backwards, limiting their leverage to negotiate for competitive salaries. They bristled at the new free agency rules, as the right of first refusal for a player's current club would even further discourage players from negotiating free agent contracts at fair market value. The reduction in years required for free agent eligibility was hardly seen as sufficient compensation. "Regardless of whether it's four years, two years or one year, a salary cap makes free agency, as we know it, pretty much eliminated," said Atlanta player rep Tom Glavine.[53] The MLBPA estimated that the

[52] Murray Chass, "Owners Unveil Salary Cap to a Chilly Reception from Players," *New York Times* June 15, 1994: B.13.
[53] Richard Justice, "Players Object to Salary Cap; No Strike Date Set; Next Meeting is July," *Washington Post* June 17, 1994: D07.

proposal would cost its members $1.5 billion in lost revenue over its 7-year lifespan.[54]

On June 18th, the MLBPA's executive director Donald Fehr announced the union's rejection of the owners' proposal. Fehr was Marvin Miller's successor, and had many of the same qualities that made Miller so successful before him. Like Miller, Fehr was in close communication with the players, earning not only their trust but their fierce loyalty. The solidarity that both men inspired was incredibly beneficial at the bargaining table, in contrast to the owners' recurring difficulty establishing a consensus among members with very different economic priorities. Also like Miller, Fehr did not run away from conflict with owners, but seemed to embrace an adversarial relationship played out in full view of the media.

---

[54] Gould, *Bargaining with Baseball,* 102-103.

Opposing him was Richard Ravitch, the lead negotiator for the Player Relations Council (PRC), the owners' bargaining group. Ravitch, a Yale Law School graduate, worked previously as the chairman of the New York Metropolitan Transit Authority. Like Fehr, Ravitch was a suitable heir to the legacy of his predecessor, the union-busting Rey Grebey who battled Miller throughout the last work stoppage in 1981. Like Grebey before him, Ravitch was similarly perceived by the union as a "hatchet man" for the owners, and Fehr scorned him publicly.[55]

Fehr and the union responded with a counter offer, rejecting a salary cap along with virtually all of the owners' requests, and proposing an increase in minimum salaries and a reduction to two years in the eligibility period for salary arbitration. In other words, it was an offer that the owners were sure to reject, but not before Fehr made the players' position known to

[55] Ross Newhan, "Ravitch Derided by Fehr," *Los Angeles Times* August 23, 1994: 1.

the media. Predictably, the union asserted that they and the owners were enormously far apart, and there was virtually no prospect of a speedy negotiation without one side giving tremendous concessions. Fehr condemned the owners and Ravitch when interviewed by Larry King, earning the two the nickname "Fehr and Loathing" for their very obvious animosity.[56] The acrimonious relationship between Fehr and Ravitch spilled over into both camps and further strained the already-remote chances of reaching a settlement without a work stoppage.

Prospects of the two sides coming together were reduced even further on August 3rd, when the owners surprisingly withheld a scheduled payment of $7.8 million that was owed to the players' pension fund after the 1994 All Star Game. The players reacted with outrage, and Donald Fehr told reporters he was "shocked beyond imagination," considering the owners'

[56] Heylar, *Lords of the Realm,* 594.

decision an act of war.57 Union counsel Gene
Orza added, "When you start playing with their
wives and children (by tampering with their
benefit plans), you've gone beyond fair play. It's
an all-time low." Some in the union even
proposed that they suspend negotiations and
strike immediately in response to the owners'
affront.58 The owners, for their part, denied
using the pension payment as a weapon. Expos
president Claude Brochu explained, "The money
to be added to the pension fund comes from the
Central Fund, and money in there is money that
comes from what are called the 'jewels' of the
game: the All-Star Game, divisional
championships and World Series. I would
presume that to the extent that both the
divisional championships and World Series

57 Murray Chass, "Brushback Pitch: Owners to Kill Pension
Payment," *New York Times* August 3, 1994: B7.
58 Ross Newhan, "Players Might Move Up Strike Date," *Los
Angeles Times* August 4, 1994: D.1

won't be played this year, then ownership is within its rights in withholding payment."[59]

Whether it was meant as an attempt to intimidate or was simply a miscommunication, the owners' decision to withhold the pension payment was an unfortunate blunder. The players, along with the media, increasingly spoke about the potential looming strike as a foregone conclusion. The owners' behavior only fanned the flames of distrust at the beginning of what looked to be a prolonged negotiation process.[60] The threat of an impending work stoppage was consistent with the pattern that emerged since the 1970s, wherein every expiring contract led to contentious negotiations and either a player strike or an owner lockout. By August 1994, the likelihood of this pattern repeating itself seemed inevitable. The only question was when.

[59] Jeff Blair, "A Last Hurrah for Walker," *The Gazette* (Montreal, QC) August 04, 1994: D1.
[60] Zimbalist, *In the Best Interests of Baseball?*, 147.

The Strike Begins

As fruitless negotiations took place periodically throughout late July and early August 1994, the MLBPA realized that the time to strike was at hand. The union had been stockpiling revenue from player licensing into a strike fund that totaled about $175 million, enough to give a player with four years experience about $150,000 to ride out a strike. By August, with more than half the season behind them, players feared that should they continue to play without coming to an agreement, owners could declare an impasse in negotiations. Federal labor laws stipulated the right of employers to make such a declaration after a reasonable interval of time elapsed without a settlement. This distressing scenario (from the union's perspective) would allow the owners to bypass collective bargaining altogether and implement their proposals unilaterally.[61] Ultimately, a mid-August strike would be the most advantageous timing from the players' perspective, having already received most of their yearly salaries. The owners, by contrast, were dependent on television revenues from the postseason to comprise a large chunk of their revenue.[62]

The MLBPA decided on an August 12th strike deadline, and the owners remained unmoved. Oakland GM Sandy Alderson likened the standoff to the summer's hit movie *Speed*: "The playoffs and World Series are the hostage; the players are driving with the explosives taped to their bodies; and the owners are the cops chasing them."[63]

On the day before the strike deadline, both Fehr and Ravitch held press conferences and appeared on local and national TV to spin their positions. "This is an action by the players,

61 Gould, *Bargaining with Baseball,* 102.
62 Heylar, *Lords of the Realm*, 595-597.
63 *Ibld.,* 597.

who under no circumstances would discuss the cost issue in baseball," Ravitch explained. "We call it collective cost; they call it a salary cap." Fehr's comments were more sardonic: "We are where we are just because the owners can't get their house together. This is a dispute between owners. It would be comical if it wasn't also so tragic."[64]

The games on August 11th were played with uncertainty in the air. As Ken Griffey hit his 40th home run of the season to seal the Mariners' 8-1 win over Oakland, it neared midnight in New York.[65] Donald Fehr was still in his office, ready for a last-minute offer that never came. The deadline arrived, and on August 12th, the players went on strike.

Attempts at Mediation with Federal Mediation and Conciliation Service

[64] Larry Whitesdale, "Bottom Line: No Settlement, So No Games," *Boston Globe* August 12, 1994: 37.
[65] Schwarz, "'94 in Review," 13.

Early in the strike, both sides agreed to enter into mediation with the Federal Mediation and Conciliation Service, such as they had done during the 1981 strike. The FMCS helped organize and direct negotiations, but lacked authority to execute binding arbitration. Its success or failure, therefore, was based on the ability and credibility of the individual mediators it provided. Several federal mediators, led by their director John Calhoun Wells, met with players and owners. On August 24, Wells filled a New York City conference room with more than twenty players, eight additional union reps, twelve owners and six of their lawyers, and four federal mediators.[66] Representatives from both sides took turns making impassioned speeches eviscerating their greedy and selfish opponents, with no useful negotiating taking place at all. On the second day, Wells adjourned the summit,

[66] Hal Bodley, "Lineup Crowded for Today's Baseball Talks," *USA Today* August 24, 1994: 01A.

having achieved nothing. Just as in 1981, the FMCS was unable to make progress toward reaching a settlement due to the resolute and inflexible stances adopted by players and owners. Wells continued to meet separately with Fehr and Ravitch in the following weeks, but was at a loss as to how to proceed, offering both sides the same message – there was no reason to meet if neither side was willing to budge.[67]

The involvement of the FMCS did make a significant impact on the negotiating dynamic in a surprising way. At the mediators' suggestion, individual owners became directly involved in the negotiations. "We should get people at the table who have considerable financial interest in baseball," said Yankees' owner George Steinbrenner. "…not a bunch of lawyers who are the only ones going to make money out of the

[67] Mark Maske, "No Talks as Hopes Keep Fading," *Washington Post* September 02, 1994: F06.

strike."[68] Inclusion of new, disparate voices at the bargaining table undercut the singular influence of Ravitch, and generated dissent and polarization among the owners' ranks.

The owners' interests in the strike were not all the same, and factions began to emerge. On one side were large-market teams like those from New York, Los Angeles, Boston, Toronto, and Atlanta, along with medium-market teams who had recently built new stadiums or were otherwise profitable, such as Colorado and Baltimore. These teams had more to lose than to gain from a protracted strike, and sought to expedite a settlement.[69]

Opposing them were the more pugnacious owners of small-market clubs, to whom a radical change was of more urgent importance. This faction included teams like Milwaukee, Minnesota, Pittsburgh, Seattle, Kansas City and San Diego. Included in their

[68] Heylar, *Lords of the Realm*, 597.
[69] *Ibid.*, 591-592.

ranks was Chicago White Sox owner Jerry Reinsdorf, who emerged as a leader among these hawkish clubs despite his team's considerable market size. Reinsdorf, one of the key accomplices in the ouster of Fay Vincent and appointment of Bud Selig, was also owner of the then-champion Chicago Bulls franchise in the NBA. That league had been operating under a salary cap since 1984, and Reinsdorf sought to apply the same principle to baseball.[70] The remaining teams did not side strongly with either faction but generally favored a moderate path to settling the strike. These mid-market teams were greater in number than the extremes on either side and were a target of constant lobbying and arm-twisting by their more strongly-opinionated peers. This polarization of owners with different economic priorities would make a settlement with the players even harder to realize, as their own rules stipulated that a

---

[70] Staudohar, *Playing for Dollars: Labor Relations and the Sports Business*, 119-121.

three-fourths majority was required to approve a settlement.71 Moreover, the owners' lack of solidarity would go on to make them far less durable than their opponents in a prolonged and costly strike.

Compounding the discord among them was the increasing number of new owners. Nine teams had been bought by new owners since the 1990 lockout, and they quickly asserted themselves among their peers. Many new owners felt entitled to speak up despite their inexperience in baseball, as they had invested huge sums of money in their new teams and were otherwise highly-respected tycoons in the outside business world. Furthermore, several of these new owners, although not present for the history of labor animosity with the MLBPA, were successful union-busters in their outside businesses. For example, the Marlins' Wayne Huizenga battled with unions as he grew Waste

71 Staudohar, "The Baseball Strike of 1994-95," 25.

Management, Inc. from the ground up, and the Royals' David Glass was CEO of the infamously union-crushing Wal-Mart, Inc. The Giants' Peter Magowan may have been the most notorious buster of all the owners: while running his Safeway grocery stores, he opted to lay off an entire 9,000-employee division altogether rather than negotiate with its troublesome union representatives. Many of these owners, with plenty of "real-world" experience but lack of familiarity with the business of baseball, quickly butted heads with the old-guard establishment.[72] The new owners would soon learn that dealing with labor that was both skilled and famous was very different than putting down unskilled Wal-Mart workers.

Colorado Rockies owner Jerry McMorris was increasingly finding a voice as a leader of the dovish owners. McMorris, like some of the more aggressive owners, had experience in the

---

[72] Heylar, *Lords of the Realm*, 593.

dynamics of labor relations, but with a more benign track record; his company, Nation's Way Transport Service, had an all-union workforce that had never gone on strike.[73] After communicating directly with Fehr throughout late August, McMorris proposed what he believed could be a viable compromise. He suggested a "luxury tax" as an alternative to a salary cap. Unlike under a cap, teams could spend as much as they wanted, but if they significantly exceeded the league average payroll, they would be taxed proportionally. These taxes would form a revenue pool that would be used to subsidize the more financially disadvantaged clubs.[74]

Many owners were wary of any deal that did not include a salary cap, but McMorris was able to sway enough of his cohorts to make a proposal that suggested a luxury tax as a feasible

[73] Mike Klis, "McMorris Gloomy After Talks Fail, Meeting with Fehr Fails to Open Discussion," *Colorado Springs Gazette-Telegraph* September 3, 1995: C5.
[74] Heylar, *Lords of the Realm*, 601.

alternative. The union received his proposal on September 2nd along with a proclamation by Selig that the remainder of the season would be cancelled if no deal was in place by September 9th. The players were skeptical of a luxury tax, which was viewed by many as merely a repackaged salary cap. "If the alternative they're willing to discuss is some other device which is essentially a salary cap but they're going to call it something else, we don't draw the distinction," Fehr told reporters.[75] The owners would be so reluctant to exceed the spending threshold, they argued, that it would keep free agent contracts under fair market value in the same way a salary cap would. Nevertheless, the union was willing to explore the possibilities of this idea, and presented a counter to the owners. The union suggested a "flat tax" of 5.25% for the top sixteen clubs by revenue and payroll, to be distributed

[75] Dave VanDyck, "Sides Headed Back to Table, Owners Indicate Salary Cap Negotiable," *Chicago Sun-Times* August 24, 1994: 96.

equally among the bottom twelve clubs, allowing poorer teams to receive subsidies without any built-in deterrent for big spending.[76] Additionally, they suggested that home teams share 25% of their gate receipts with visiting teams across the entire sport. Under the current model, American League home teams were sharing 20% of gate receipts with visiting clubs, while National League teams were sharing only 5% with visitors.[77]

The owners rejected the union's flat tax proposal, and as the deadline to save what remained of the season approached, no end to the strike was in sight. At Selig's prompting, twenty-six of the twenty-eight owners faxed in votes supporting the resolution to abort the rest of the season.[78] Baltimore's Peter Angelos, a staunch member of the pacifist group, abstained,

[76] Zimbalist, *In the Best Interests of Baseball?*, 147.
[77] Staudohar, "The Baseball Strike of 1994-95," 24.
[78] Heylar, *Lords of the Realm*, 602-603.

along with the enduringly clueless Marge
Schott.[79]

On September 14th , Bud Selig sat before
the press and declared the 1994 season officially
abandoned, including the cancellation of the
1994 World Series. "We ran out of ground," Selig
said. "It's tragic, but I wasn't going to allow the
most important games of the season to become a
farce." He continued, "There are no winners in
this. Both sides failed on so many fronts. I mean,
it's almost impossible to articulate the sense of
sadness and poignancy I feel today." Donald
Fehr's response to Selig's emotional display was
predictably disdainful: "This is the result they
anticipated all along. I'm amazed by the

---

[79] Schott, owner of the Cincinnati Reds, was only recently
back in the owners' fold after serving a one-year
suspension for making a variety of racially inflammatory
remarks. Schott blustered that she believed the wisest
course of action was to immediately resume the season
using minor league players.

equanimity with which they've tossed away the season."[80]

The last time a World Series had been cancelled was in 1904, when the New York Giants refused to risk their National League Championship by taking part in a then-optional game with the American League champion Boston club. Giants manager John McGraw, involved in a bitter feud with the American League and its President Ban Johnson, convinced owner John T. Brush to declare that his team would not "submit its championship honors to a contest with a victorious club of a minor league." Sportswriters and fans responded with harsh criticism, and a public backlash ensued. Brush realized that he had not only misjudged how fans would react, but also the lucrative opportunity that a championship series would have provided.

[80] Ross Newhan, "Baseball Season, Series Cancelled: Owners Say Failure to Reach Bargaining Accord and 34-Day Players' Strike Made it Impossible to Resume Play," *Los Angeles Times* September 15, 1994: 1.

In response, Brush helped write new rules for postseason play that compelled both league winners to play at the end of the season, and in 1905, the World Series was established as an annual baseball tradition.[81] That tradition continued unbroken for the next 89 years, until the 1994 strike. Once again, owners underestimated the extent of disappointment, outrage and disgust that would define baseball fans' response. This time, the fans would be even less forgiving.

Presidential and Congressional Involvement

As the stalemate continued through October, President Bill Clinton became increasingly frustrated by the ineffectiveness of the Federal Mediation and Conciliation Service thus far. Clinton appointed a new mediator,

[81] Morris, *A Game of Inches,* 431-432.

William J. Usery, Jr., to help resolve the strike. Usery had previously served as director of the FMCS and as Secretary of Labor under President Gerald Ford, spending his time afterwards as an effective freelance mediator in several large labor disputes involving Eastern Airlines and Pittston Coal. At 70 years old, he seemed to bring the experience, persistence, and knowledge that this particularly challenging situation demanded. Usery was able to eke out some cooperation from both sides, and a consensus emerged that some form of revenue redistribution from rich to poor teams would be a feature of whatever agreement they would eventually reach. Ultimately, though, Usery was unable to bridge the gap between players and owners in any significant way. The MLBPA's position remained steadfast against any limitation on player salaries; they were willing to see teams redistribute revenues on their own, but not at their expense. The owners continued to squabble among themselves, unable to reach a consensus.[82]

One thing the owners did agree on after meeting with Usery was the decision to orchestrate the replacement of Richard Ravitch as the PRC's lead negotiator. Ravitch was increasingly marginalized by Selig until his influence was almost negligible, and he announced his resignation in early December. Into his place stepped more moderate Boston owner John Harrington, a member of the ascending faction that included McMorris.[83]

On December 20th, the owners declared an impasse in negotiations. They argued that an excessive amount of time had passed without any real good-faith offers of compromise by the players, and they had to proceed with making arrangements for the 1995 season. Thus, the owners' proposals, including a salary cap, were unilaterally put into effect. The union objected

[82] Staudohar, *Playing for Dollars,* 50-51.
[83] Zimbalist, *In the Best Interests of Baseball?,* 148.

and filed an unfair labor practice charge with the National Labor Relations Board (NLRB).

In late January 1995, an annoyed President Clinton issued an ultimatum. Clinton indicated that if a settlement was not reached by February 7th, he would ask William Usery to draw up his own plan for a settlement. Of course, Usery and the FMCS had no binding authority, but the President intimated that his recommendations would either be forwarded to Congress as the basis for legislative intervention, or used as the basis for arbitration.[84] "Clearly, they are not capable of settling this without an umpire," Clinton told the press. "The only way to do this appears to be for Congress to step up to the plate and pass the legislation." Clinton invited both sides to the White House on the day of his deadline, where he, along with Vice President Gore and Chief of Staff Leon Panetta,

[84] Gould, *Bargaining with Baseball,* 104-105.

met for hours with owners and players. Despite Clinton's best efforts, a settlement was not reached. Usery issued some suggestions, including a luxury tax, but wasn't even able to bring the sides together enough to issue a formal recommendation before the deadline. Gene Orza subsequently blasted Usery in the media, calling him "senile."[85]

Unfortunately for Clinton, Congress was not willing or able to hold up its end of the bargain, either. In a joint statement issued by House Speaker Newt Gingrich and Senate Majority Leader Bob Dole, the congressional leaders expressed reluctance to become involved in mediating the strike: "The president has apparently thrown the ball into Congress' court. We maintain our view that Congress is ill-suited to resolving private labor disputes."[86] With

[85] Michael Bevans, "Let's Make a Deal," *Sports Illustrated* February 20, 1995.
[86] William Neikirk, "His Baseball Jawboning Fails, So Clinton Turns to Congress," *Chicago Tribune* February 08, 1997.

Congress uninterested in participating, Clinton's threat of legislation was nullified. As for submitting to arbitration, both players and owners refused to take the risk of a binding arbitration that had the potential of going against their favor. Clinton's attempt at heavy-handed wielding of executive power to mediate a "square deal" resolution was a failure. The mood surrounding the negotiations was gloomier than ever: "I was always optimistic through this entire process, but I've never been as frustrated or as disappointed as I was after what happened in Washington," Jerry McMorris told *Sports Illustrated*. "I still feel that way. I don't see any signs now that it's going to change."[87]

While Congressional legislation to end baseball's labor dispute seemed unlikely, several congressmen attempted to expedite a resolution to the strike through different channels. In February 1995, Senators Orrin Hatch, Daniel

[87] Bevans, "Let's Make a Deal."

Patrick Moynihan, and Bob Graham introduced a bill to attack MLB's antitrust exemption. The bill did not reverse the exemption directly, but it would have allowed the players to sue the owners if they unilaterally implemented new work rules in the event of a negotiating impasse, such as they had threatened to do before the players' preemptive strike. The bill was designed not to end the strike outright, but to pressure owners to reach a settlement out of fear of litigation. Donald Fehr promised that if the bill was passed, the players would end their strike, but predicted the owners would initiate a lockout once they returned to work.[88] Despite these assurances, Congress voted, and the pro-labor bill was not passed.

The President and Congress were both unable to force an end to the strike; it would be another avenue of government involvement that would eventually bring the strike to an end, but

[88] Murray Chass, "Hatch Hopeful on Antitrust Repeal," *New York Times* February 14, 1995: B.10.

that was still several months away. In the meantime, as the winter of 1995 came to a close with no resolution on the horizon, owners began to weigh their options for the upcoming 1995 season. They made it clear that spring training would take place with or without the striking players. Figuring out who would take their place, however, would be problematic.

Replacement Players

The owners had already voted to authorize the use of so-called replacement players on January 13, 1995. The union retorted that these "scabs" were not replacements at all, since the MLBPA's striking players were still under contract. In any event, the owners' use of these strikebreakers would be their first attempt since the Detroit players' one-day strike in 1912 to pass off teams of semi-professionals as the genuine article.

Not all owners supported the use of strikebreakers. Baltimore owner Peter Angelos, a labor lawyer, refused to use them for his club. Angelos told *Sports Illustrated*, "to expect major league fans to accept less than major league baseball is unrealistic and, I believe, will ultimately prove to be foolhardy. These are the best players in the world. There are no replacements. That's a hallucination."[89] Additionally, Angelos was disinclined to undermine his star Cal Ripken's streak of consecutive games played, as Ripken was on the brink of breaking Lou Gherig's record of 2,130.[90] Finally, Angelos, having only just bought the team in 1993, went on a spending spree that year, acquiring several high-priced players including Rafael Palmeiro, Sid Fernandez, and Chris Sabo. Palmerio and Ripken were the fourth and fifth highest paid players in the game respectively, on whom Angelos invested a combined $10.8 million in 1994 alone.[91] He was hardly eager to see his newly acquired stars be replaced by minor leaguers and journeymen. American League president Gene Bundig responded initially to Angelos' defiance with threat of forfeiture, referring to section 3.8 of the

[89] Tim Kurkjian, "Throwing Curves," *Sports Illustrated* January 09, 1995.
[90] Zimbalist, *May the Best Team Win,* 90.
[91] Schwarz, "'94 in Review," 9, 19.

AL constitution which gave the league power to "terminate membership" for "willfully violating... any order of the president," or "any act, omission, transaction or conduct found by the league not to be in the best interests of baseball."[92] Bundig prudently decided against any attempt to confiscate the team, instead making an agreement with Angelos that the Orioles would simply forfeit any scheduled replacement games, allowing Ripken's streak to remain intact.[93]

Complicating matters further were labor laws in Ontario and Quebec that barred management from using picket-crossing strikebreakers in just such a circumstance, rendering the Toronto and Montreal clubs unable to host games using replacement

[92] Associated Press, "Baseball Owners Claim Union Threatening Replacement Players," *Ottawa Citizen* (Ottawa, ON) January 19, 1995: D8.
[93] Mark Maske, "At the Ol' (Replacement) Ball Game," *Washington Post* March 26, 2995: A1.

players.94 Blue Jays management came up with a plan to use their spring training facility in Dunedin, Florida, to play their regular season home games. The stadium, regularly used by Dunedin High School, seated a mere 6,128 and had subpar lighting that would require all Toronto's games there to be played during daylight hours.95 Luckily, Blue Jays fans would never be forced to make the 1,300-plus mile journey.

Spring Training opened inconspicuously in 1995, with minor league players showing up as they normally do every year. The players who reported were not necessarily "scabs" from the union's perspective, as only a select few minor leaguers who filled out the big clubs' 40-man rosters were members of the union. Minor league players were not forced to cross a literal or figurative picket line when training camp

94 Russ Cohen with Nikco Riesgo, *Strike Three: A Player's Journey through the Infamous Baseball Strike of 1994* (Raleigh, HC: Lulu.com, 2009), 3-4.
95 Maske, "At the Ol' (Replacement) Ball Game."

began. For the first few weeks, players went through the motions of camp and inter-squad games without knowing if they would be sent back down to the minors for more seasoning or called upon to play in spring training games, thereby filling a striking player's roster spot. It was at this juncture that minor league players were forced to make a difficult decision: the union declared that any player who participated in a regularly scheduled spring training exhibition game or any other game for which admission was charged would be considered a strikebreaker. Owners argued that minor leaguers have always appeared in spring training games, to which Donald Fehr retorted, "In the past, nonroster players might occasionally play in such games along major leaguers, but it was not the presence of the nonroster players that made those games major league exhibition games. It was the presence of the major leaguers that did, and this year the major leaguers are on strike."[96] The line was drawn, with the first exhibition games scheduled to begin on March 2nd.

To play as a strikebreaker meant being forever labeled a "scab" by their fellow players if and when the strike ended. Angels pitcher and player rep Mark Langston told reporters that the players "occupying" clubhouses were "totally living in a dream world." Langston continued, "I don't know when they're going to wake up and realize none of them are considered prospects... they've only been hired to undermine something we believe in. If they can look in the mirror and say they're proud of what they're doing, then obviously their intestinal fortitude is not as strong as it should be."[97] The Mets' Bobby Bonilla put it more succinctly when he threatened that

[96] Jim Litke, "Union Cautions Minor Leaguers, Players Warn Spring 'Scabs'," *The Commercial Appeal* (Memphis, TN) February 23, 1995: D.2.
[97] Mike DiGiovanna, "Langston Has Harsh Words for Fill-Ins," *Los Angeles Times* March 7, 1995.

any player who crossed the picket line might "end up in the East River."[98]

However, Bonilla was, after all, the highest-paid player in the game. For struggling minor leaguers, the call for replacement players was a potential once-in-a-lifetime opportunity to advance their careers and provide for their families. Many, such as Expos minor league outfielder Nikco Riesgo, decided to accept offers to play based on frustration with a journeyman career that never materialized as he had hoped and the financial pressure that went along with years spent toiling in the minors.[99] For most unheralded minor league players, the choice to sign on was an easy one. The strikebreakers were signed to a standard contract of $115,000, the league-wide minimum salary under the system the owners unilaterally implemented in December. Since the contracts were obviously

---

[98] Rick Telander, "A Minor Adjustment," *Sports Illustrated* November 21, 1994.
[99] Cohen and Riesgo, *Strike Three*, 5-6.

not guaranteed, players were paid 1/183rd of their salary for each day they remained on team rosters, or $628.42 per day.[100]

Clubs varied in their philosophies regarding exactly which minor leaguers should sign on as replacement players. Some demanded total participation, with Cincinnati general manager Jim Bowden informing all the team's minor leaguers that those who refuse to play would be released.[101] Other organizations such as the San Francisco Giants took the opposite approach, creating a separate "minicamp" for its top prospects to shield them from the messiness of the entire fiasco.[102] Most teams, however, struggled to balance the immediate need to field a replacement team with the long-term development of the club's prospects. "There is a clause in their [minor-league] contracts that says

[100] Ronald Blum, "Baseball Seeks Job Applicants," *York Daily Record* (York, PA) January 14, 1995.
[101] Jayson Stark, "Minor Leaguers Facing Major Quandary," *Philadelphia Inquirer* February 20, 1995: C.1.
[102] Larry Stone, "Giants Don Kid Gloves to Handle 2 Camps in 1," *San Francisco Examiner* February 16, 1995: D.1.

they must play in major-league exhibition games if they're asked, and if they don't, they're 'disqualified'," said Phillies president Bill Giles. "But I don't think we'd ever do that. It's kind of senseless to disqualify somebody you're trying to develop as a major-leaguer." Instead of pressuring top prospects to cross the picket line, Giles was content with filling roster spots with players like journeyman minor-league catcher Joe Cipolloni, who spent the seven years since he last played professionally working in a South Philly pizzeria.[103]

In addition to hopeful youngsters, many aged veterans also reported with training camp invitations in 1995, hoping to reignite their careers. Gorman Thomas, veteran of a thirteen-year career, hit 45 home runs in 1979 and tied with Reggie Jackson for the home run title in 1982 with 39. Now age 44, Thomas felt like he had little to lose by accepting an invitation from

[103] Stark, "Minor Leaguers Facing Major Quandary," C.1.

his former club in Milwaukee and giving his
career another go, despite not playing in a major
league game since 1986.[104]

Like Thomas, former Red Sox pitcher
Dennis "Oil Can" Boyd saw an invitation to White
Sox training camp as a shot at the major leagues
he would be unable to get otherwise. Boyd, age
35, had been out of the league since 1991, and
sought redemption for a career he felt was cut
short by unfair treatment in the wake of several
clubhouse outbursts and brushes with the law.
"In my heart, I know no man paid dues like I did
to get to the major leagues except Jackie
Robinson," he explained to clubhouse reporters.
Not surprisingly, Boyd was a lightning rod for
criticism by players loyal to the union, who
pointed out that the union's support allowed him
to make big money during his once-successful
career. Boyd's arrival at training camp in a red
Mercedes convertible with vanity license plates

[104] Cohen and Riesgo, *Strike Three*, 6-7.

reading "OIL CAN" only served to emphasize this point. Joining Boyd at White Sox training camp was NBA superstar Michael Jordan, in the midst of an unsuccessful attempt to break into a second sport. Jordan, though, was careful to make his role in spring training clear: "I'm strictly a minor leaguer....I'm not here to try to take someone's job when they're not here."[105] When Jordan's very accommodating boss, Chicago Bulls and White Sox owner Jerry Reinsdorf, made a visit to training camp, he commended the replacements who were there for refusing to blindly follow the Players Association and Donald Fehr. "Don't believe the owners, but for God's sake, this isn't Guyana. Don't believe the guy that's misleading you," he told players, whimsically equating Fehr to murder-suicide cult leader Jim Jones.[106]

A few striking major league players even flirted with the idea of crossing the picket line

[105] Mark Maske, "'Oil' and 'Air' Are an Odd Mix in Spring Camp," *Washington Post* February 19, 1995: D.01.
[106] "Poll Indicates Game is Losing Fans' Support," *Sun Sentinel* (Fort Lauderdale, FL) March 27, 1995.

and becoming labeled scabs themselves. Astros pitcher Greg Swindell told reporters, "I have very few friends in baseball right now that I'm close and personal with anyway... I've got house payments, I've got ex-wife payments, I've got a five-year-old, a three-year-old and a seven-week-old. So it's a tough decision."[107] Swindell was in the minority in expressing any doubts in the strike, with the vast majority of players publicly maintaining conviction in their cause. Ultimately though, neither Swindell nor any other active major leaguer would cross the picket line.

Detroit Tigers manager Sparky Anderson refused to work with replacement players, telling reporters, "I always wondered if something really important came up, could I stand up? I didn't know. I'd never had to. This time, I had to. What [baseball owners] are doing

107 Tim Kurkjian, "Throwing Curves," *Sports Illustrated* January 09, 1995.

with replacement players is ridiculous."108 As the only manager in the sport who took such a stance, Anderson's objection was not based on belief in solidarity with the players' cause, but dedication to the integrity of baseball itself: "[The games] don't belong to the owners with all their power and all the money that they made from all their other businesses," he would go on to write, reflecting on the incident in his 1998 memoir. "They don't belong to the players who make a million dollars a month. Some of these guys walk around like they're doing the fans a favor just by showing up to the park. The games belong to the fans."109 Tigers owner Mike Ilitch, one of baseball's "new owners" whose corporate management style already clashed with Anderson's old-school view of the game, placed

108 Joe Leyden, *The Great American Baseball Strike* (Brookfield, CT: Millbrook Press, 1995), 45-47.
109 Sparky Anderson with Dan Ewald, *They Call Me Sparky* (Chelsea, MI: Sleeping Bear Press, 1998), 247.

the manager on an involuntary unpaid leave of absence.110

Other managers' responses varied. Cincinnati Reds manager Davey Johnson called replacement baseball "a travesty" to reporters, but was effectively muzzled when team ownership threatened his job in response.111 Dodgers manager Tommy Lasorda, unlike most of his peers, embraced the challenge of working with replacements with downright enthusiasm. Rejuvenated by working with these fresh-faced green recruits, Lasorda explained, "The other guys (major-league managers) don't enjoy it, but the thing with me is I'm enjoying it because it's an opportunity to teach youngsters." Not wanting his excitement to be held against him

110 John Lowe, "The Passing of a Legend," *Sparky Anderson: The Life of a Baseball Legend,* eds. Tom Panzenhagen and Barry Forbis (Chicago: Triumph Books, 2010): 29-30.
111 Maske, "At the Ol' (Replacement) Ball Game."

when the major leaguers returned, he added, "If I've got to do it, I'm going to do it and enjoy it."[112] Fans, however, were less enthusiastic. Spring training games with replacement players began, and, as Angels beat reporter Jeff Miller wrote, "some had forecast unrest and hostility. The actual feeling... was closer to placid indifference."[113] An AP poll reported that 38% of baseball fans said they would watch fewer games with replacement players, and 28% expected their interest to remain diminished even after the strike's end.[114] As spring training continued, attendance decreased, down by as much as 60% for teams such as the Boston Red Sox.[115] Television advertisers echoed fan apathy and

[112] Ken Dailey, "Skipper is Chiper: Lasorda Misses Players but Has Rapt Audience," *Daily News* (Los Angeles) March 21, 1995: S1.

[113] Jeff Miller, "A Winning Day for Replacement Fan," *Orange County Register* (Santa Ana, CA) March 2, 1995: A01.

[114] Associated Press, "More Baseball Fans Vowing to Skip Replacement Games," *Salt Lake Tribune* March 27, 1995: C2.

[115] Maske, "At the Ol' (Replacement) Ball Game."

largely chose to stay away from buying time on replacement game broadcasts. A Midas Muffler representative told reporters, "We're in business. We're real. Replacement baseball isn't."[116] Consequently, broadcasters such as New York's Madison Square Garden network, television partner of the New York Yankees, refused to air spring training games due to "virtually no interest from the advertising community."[117] Further complicating things, as an MSG executive explained, was dealing with organized labor: "A lot [of the TV networks] have unions and if they buy time, they'd look like they're crossing picket lines."[118]

While replacement players were accepted by some, the Players Association understandably abhorred their existence. In fact, the union announced on March 16th that it would

116 Barry Cooper, "Advertisers Aren't Buying Replacement Baseball," *Oakland Post* (Oakland, CA) March 8, 1995: 11.
117 Maske, "At the Ol' (Replacement) Ball Game."
118 Cooper, "Advertisers Aren't Buying Replacement Baseball."

absolutely not agree to a settlement in which replacement games were counted in the standings and "scab" players' statistics were included in baseball's official records. Union executive Gene Orza described the issue as a "line in the sand," on which the players would not compromise. "Suppose a guy hits four home runs off a 53-year-old pitcher. Should he be up there with Mike Schmidt and Lou Gherig on the all-time list? This isn't major league baseball. It's a fantasy camp." The owners' response was equally inflexible: "We would never agree to expunge games and records," a management lawyer told the press. "If you're saying the games don't count, fans would be justified in asking for their money back. There's just no chance of it happening. If the season starts with replacement players, the games will count."[119] As the season's scheduled start date of April 2nd rapidly

[119] Ross Newhan, "Players Draw the Line Against Replacement Games, Records," *Los Angeles Times March* 16, 1995: 3.

approached, the prospect of playing regular-season games with replacement players grew increasingly untenable. Nevertheless, both players and owners were prepared for exactly such a scenario. Fortunately, an end to the strike would come sooner and more abruptly than either side anticipated.

National Labor Relations Board

The MLBPA filed a grievance with the National Labor Relations Board in December, 1994, in response to the owners' unilateral implementation of a salary cap. The owners' decision was predicated on the idea that an impasse had been reached, since two whole years had passed since they opened negotiations in December 1992. The players protested, pointing out that negotiations were opened in

December 1992 but the owners had failed to
make an actual proposal until 18 months later.
Furthermore, the owners advocated drastic
alterations to the agreement, and refused to
change their proposals in response to player
counteroffers. A second grievance was filed in
February after owners made further unilateral
decisions to revoke salary arbitration.[120] The
players' unfair labor practice complaints to the
NLRB stated that there was no impasse and that
it was the owners, not the players, who were
failing to negotiate in good faith. Now, the
players argued, the owners were attempting to
bypass the collective bargaining process
altogether, violating federal labor law.

In March 1995, the NLRB read the
players' grievances, and the five-member board
met for a vote to determine their ruling. Their
decision would determine the fate of Major
League Baseball.

[120] Zimbalist, *In the Best Interests of Baseball?*, 149.

CHAPTER 3: Aftermath

As the 1995 baseball season loomed ahead, along with the very real possibility of official Major League games played by semi-pro strikebreakers, the MLBPA made a last-ditch appeal to the National Labor Relations Board. Their complaint described unreasonable behavior by Major League Baseball's owners, who refused to negotiate in good faith and sought to unilaterally implement radical changes to the collective bargaining agreement, in violation of federal labor law. In March 1995, The NLRB's five members met to respond to the players' allegations and render a decision that would decide the future of the game.

NLRB Injunction – The Strike Ends

The NLRB's Chairman William Gould was an unabashed baseball devotee and a former mediator in Major League Baseball salary arbitration cases. Gould was not without his critics, who suggested his fandom could create a potential conflict of interest.121 Nevertheless, Gould, an appointee of President Clinton, found himself in a unique position to make his mark on the history of the game he loved. The NLRB convened on March 26, 1995, and voted 3-2 in the players' favor, determining to seek a court injunction that would force the owners to reestablish the terms of the old collective bargaining agreement. An excited Donald Fehr told the media that should such an injunction restore the terms of the old collective bargaining agreement, the players would end the strike and

121 Gould, *Bargaining with Baseball,* 100-102.

return to work.122 This alone would not guarantee an end to the work stoppage, as the owners could simply initiate a lockout in response. The owners would, however, need a three-fourths majority vote to do so, which seemed an unlikely prospect at this late and weary stage of the strike.

On March 31, 1995, Manhattan District Court Judge Sonya Sotomayor heard the case. Representatives for the owners argued that the areas in which they made unilateral changes were not subject to collective bargaining, and thus they were free to take such action. Sotomayor, however, stated that any provision that affected wages was indeed subject to collective bargaining, and this was a category under which the owners' actions fell. Putting her support squarely behind the players, she waxed poetic about the cultural significance of the

122 Ronald Blum, "Fehr Has New Offer for Teams," *Pittsburgh Post-Gazette* March 30, 1995: D1.

game: "Opening Day is one of the most beautiful days on the baseball calendar and it should not be disturbed because one side has failed to fulfill its duties under the collective bargaining mandates of this country."[123] The court issued an injunction that forced a restoration of all the terms and conditions of the old contract. Further, Sotomayor ordered both sides back to the bargaining table, and mandated that the owners could not impose any new set of working conditions without first appearing before her in court once again.[124]

For the players, it was an irrefutable victory. The ruling "provided every bit of relief we asked for," said Fehr, and on April 2nd, as promised, the Players Association made an unconditional offer to the owners to end the strike.[125] The owners met to decide whether or not to lock out the players, but a growing

[123] Lowenfish, *The Imperfect Diamond,* 294-295.
[124] Gould, *Bargaining with Baseball,* 108.
[125] Ross Newhan, "Baseball Players Offer to End 232-Day Strike," *Los Angeles Times* April 1, 1995: 1.

number of owners in favor of a settlement clearly negated the possibility of reaching the three-fourths majority needed for a lockout. The decision was made to accept the players' offer without even taking a vote. It was time, the owners realized, to admit defeat. "The players are back, the game is back, and we are very happy about it," Bud Selig insisted. "We hope to resolve our differences so that we and our fans never have to go through the heartache we have endured the last eight months."[126]

Apart from compassion for the fans, the decision to refrain from a lockout was certainly influenced by fear that such a move could be subject to court action. If they went ahead with a lockout only to have it subsequently ruled illegal, it would not only spoil the owners' efforts but leave them on the hook for back pay with interest, amounting up to $1 billion for a full

[126] John Delcos, "Baseball Enters Home Stretch," *York Daily Record* (York, PA) April 3, 1995: 01.

season.[127] This fear would later be confirmed when the Second Court of Appeals emphatically upheld Sotomayor's decision.[128]

After a few weeks of delayed spring training, a shortened season of 144 games was set to begin on April 26th. The idea of baseball's triumphant return was met with mixed reactions. Kansas City pitcher and player representative David Cone was enthusiastic: "It's nice to be talking about putting on a uniform. I haven't had much time to work out. I've been going to these damn meetings... The players are ready to go."[129] When the season's first game finally arrived, a Tuesday night contest between the Dodgers and Marlins, both teams lined up along the base paths and tipped their caps in a

[127] Rick Hummell, "Baseball Lockout Unlikely: Owners Postpone Season Opener, Send Replacement Players Packing," *St. Louis Post-Dispatch* April 2, 1995: 01.A.
[128] Alan Schwarz, "'95 in Review," *Baseball America 1996 Almanac*, ed. Allan Simpson (Durham, NC: Baseball America, 1996), 6-8.
[129] Mark Maske, "Baseball Players Offer to End Strike; Federal Judge Rules Against Owners," *Washington Post* April 01, 1995.

gesture of apology to the fans of South Florida. The sellout crowd booed them loudly.[130] Several in the stands wore paper bags on their heads with "fan on strike" written boldly across the front. When interviewed by reporters, the man who printed and distributed the bags responded, "What can I say? I love the game of baseball. I'm still on strike. It's just a strike deep inside."[131] After the game, Dodgers' third baseman Tim Wallach was contrite: "We all took it for granted that everything would be fine once we got all that other stuff settled. Well, obviously, that wasn't the case. People are definitely upset about what happened, and they have every right to be."[132]

[130] Associated Press, "Balls & Strikes Replace Strike, Opener Lets Baseball Fans Forgive," *Salt Lake Tribune*, April 26, 1995: B.1.
[131] Jayson Stark, "Finally, Baseball Opens '95 Season," *Philadelphia Inquirer* April 26, 1995: D.1.
[132] *Ibid.*

The Damage Done: The Season that Could Have Been

The strike-shortened 1994 season left many fans and players disappointed, as numerous key opportunities for on-field success vanished. Ken Griffey Jr., asked about the untimely ending to outstanding seasons he and Chicago White Sox slugger Frank Thomas were having, remarked, "We picked a bad year to have a good year."[133] Among those to have promising individual seasons cut short was Tony Gwynn, who was in the midst of an attempt to hit .400 for the first time since Ted Williams batted .406 in 1941. Gwynn was batting .394 when the strike began, and had 18 games remaining against the mediocre pitching staffs of the Cardinals, Cubs, Marlins and Rockies. "It could have been a dream season," lamented Gwynn in

[133] E.M. Swift and Richard O'Brien, "They Said It," *Sports Illustrated* August 22, 1994.

an interview. "But the issues are more important," he added, ever a union stalwart.[134]

San Francisco Giants slugger Matt Williams hit 43 home runs at the '94 season's end, and was steadily progressing toward Roger Maris's single season record of 61 home runs. In fact, with his 43rd home run in 115 games, Williams was on exact pace to match Maris's 1961 campaign.[135] Houston's Jeff Bagwell won the 1994 NL MVP award, but missed a chance to truly have a season for the ages: he hit .368, and had the year played out, was on pace to hit an impressive 57 home runs with 166 RBI.[136]

The Montreal Expos were hit especially hard by the strike. When the 1994 season ended, the Expos stood in first place with a record of 74-40 and a shot at the playoffs in hand. The team,

[134] Tim Kurkjian, "Star Bursts," *Sports Illustrated* September 26, 1994.
[135] Robert McG Thomas, Jr., "Baseball: If It's Over, '94 Season Had Tight Races and Individual Accomplishments," *New York Times* August 12, 1994: B11.
[136] Tim Kurkjian, "Star Bursts," *Sports Illustrated* September 26, 1994.

built upon homegrown talent, maintained success despite the game's second-lowest payroll ($18.6 million), less than half that of the National League's top-spending Atlanta Braves ($40.5 million).[137] The club saw their aspirations for success cut short upon the termination of the season, much to the disappointment of the team's already-small fan base. The reinstatement of the previous CBA rendered team ownership unable to afford to keep many of their star players, or so they claimed, and most were traded off to more financially resourceful clubs. As the team's performance on the field declined accordingly, attendance and public interest lagged. Ownership found itself unable to secure a deal to build a new ballpark that would allow them to leave the supposedly problematic Olympic Stadium, further exacerbating the club's woes. By 2005, the team was relocated and rechristened the Washington Nationals. While

[137] Tim Kurkjian, "Baseball: Expo Economics," *Sports Illustrated* August 8, 1994.

other factors certainty contributed to the Expos'
downfall, a successful playoff run by the
promising 1994 squad certainly could have gone
a long way in building a future for Québécois
baseball. However, it was not to be, and the
Expos franchise remains arguably one of the
more tragic victims of the strike.138

As for the so-called replacement players,
all were released immediately as part of the
agreement to return to work in the wake of
Sotomayor's injunction. Commissioner Selig
thanked the strikebreakers for "interrupting
their lives to help us out," and the big-league
hopefuls found their dreams abruptly shattered.
Most returned to a life of obscurity, but a few of
the more promising strikebreakers managed to
find their way onto big league rosters after the
strike. Nineteen such players in total were
signed to major league rosters for the 1995
season and most were thoroughly ostracized by

---

138 Stu Cowan, "There Just Weren't Enough 'Real' Baseball
Fans Here," *The Gazette* (Montreal, QC) April 24, 2005: C5.

their teammates. Dodgers rookie third baseman and former strikebreaker Mike Busch was famously shunned on national television, forced to sit alone on the bench during what should have been a joyful major league debut.[139] With time, clubhouse attitudes toward the "scabs" mellowed and some former strikebreakers eventually gained acceptance among teammates, but were never fully forgiven. First baseman Kevin Millar, a key contributor to the 2004 World Series-champion Boston Red Sox was one such player, along with a trio of players featured in 2000's "Subway Series": New York Yankees' outfielder Shane Spencer, and the New York Mets' Rick Reed and Benny Agbayani. Despite their achievements, however, the Players Association barred these players and all former strikebreakers from union membership, officially designating them Non-Union Replacement Players. They could not share in its licensing

[139] Schwarz, "'95 in Review," 7.

revenues, nor have their names or likenesses used on officially licensed memorabilia.[140]

The Damage Done: Public Reactions

The 1994-95 strike is noteworthy for the particularly strong negative fan response it provoked. In previous work stoppages, the generally accepted narrative was one of an antagonistic party (usually the owners) battling against an innocent opponent. To wit, the 1981 strike, despite being tagged as "The Walkout the Owners Provoked" by one *Sports Illustrated* cover-story headline, was certainly met with a fairly negative fan reaction. According to a survey commissioned by MLB, 29% of self-identified baseball fans polled sided with the clubs and 17% with the players, while the majority, the remaining 54%, remaining uncommitted to either side. Overall, most fans

---

[140] Lowenfish, *The Imperfect Diamond*, 295.

simply wanted baseball to continue,

uninterrupted.141 Despite the indignation it

aroused, the calamity of the 1981 strike would

be dwarfed by the sheer cataclysm of the conflict

that succeeded it.

In contrast, the 1994 strike, unlike prior

work stoppages, was perceived as a product of

greed on both sides – stamped with the slug line

"millionaires fighting with billionaires" – with

fans as the innocent victims, and the institution

of baseball itself (in the modern, not historical,

sense) as the antagonist.

Surveys of public opinion during the

strike yielded responses ranging between

disappointment, anger, cynicism, and dejected

apathy. "I've heard a lot about what's in the best

interest of the owners or players," one fan told a

New York Times reporter. "Nobody's talking

about what's in the best interests of the game or

141 Lieberman Research Inc., "How Baseball Fans Feel
About A Possible Strike," Bowie K Kuhn Collection, BA MSS
100, National Baseball Hall of Fame & Museum
(Cooperstown, NY): March, 1980.

the fans." Said another, "They've been on strike so long, I'm kind of glad they're going to cancel [The World Series], since both sides will be hurt, not just the fans. They'll not only lose money, but interest in the future." A fan in the Bronx told a reporter frankly, "I can say that the last baseball game I ever attended was Phil Rizzuto night at Yankee Stadium a couple of days before the strike. I'm not going to be a part of the baseball picture any more." A Long Island man simply expressed apathy: "I don't really care anymore," he said. "I get up and go to work in the morning. They deserve each other. The rest of the world still goes around."[142] Fans elsewhere around the country voiced sentiments of their own. A few examples:

> Both the player and owners wrongly assume that fans have bottomless pockets to pay for tickets, for food and souvenirs at the ballpark…At a time when attending a ball game is growing out of reach for the

[142] Robert McG Thomas, Jr., "Baseball: The Fans; Booooooo! Crowd Doesn't Like Call," *New York Times* September 15, 1994: B12.

average fan, it is difficult to feel compassion for either side. – Michael A. Kirsh, Tenafly, NJ.

Most pro athletes are unappreciative, overpaid jocks who live like royalty at the expense of the fans. If the players thought for one minute that the fans would not return, a strike would not have been considered. This is one fan who will not be back. Wake up, Boys of Summer, you need us, but we don't need you. – David M. Faulk, Enterprise, AL.

Pity the fans in San Francisco who won't be watching Matt Williams chase Roger Maris's home run record. Be disgusted that the people in Chicago won't be rooting for Frank Thomas to become the first Triple Crown winner in 27 years. Mourn for the fans in San Diego who won't get to pull for Tony Gywnn to match Ted Williams's feat of hitting .400. Feel sorry for the workers in all the stadiums who are laid off. But don't feel sorry for the players. They have matched the owners in their greed and lack of respect for the game. – Kenn Auenevoli, Florissant, MO.[143]

[143] All quoted in "Letters," *Sports Illustrated* August 29, 1994.

Passionate observers struggled to comprehend how sums of money so great could be insufficient for anyone, let alone their heroes. *New York Times* writer Claire Smith asked, "Why could 700 players and 28 owners not set aside issues of power, greed and ego long enough to divide a multibillion-dollar pie?" She continued, "But don't believe for a moment there are innocent parties. There are only innocent victims, especially the thousands who lost their jobs at ballparks and do not have the safety nets that strike funds and hoarded revenues give the players and owners."[144] A fan from Tennessee echoed that sentiment in letter to the editor of *Sports Illustrated*: "This is the same group of spoiled millionaires who crossed the umpires' picket line this spring and in the past have

[144] Claire Smith, "Take 700 Players and 28 Owners and It Winds Up to 0 Solution," *New York Times* September 15, 1994: B13.

ignored strikes by concession workers... Thank god football is here!"[145]

Calls for general boycotts by the fans were common. "A fan boycott of all major league games when they resume would show both sides who really controls the finances," writes a fan from Arizona.[146] "They take our money, but they take us for suckers, and they take us for granted," declared sportswriter Steve Wulf. "I'm mad as hell and I'm not going to take – or give – any more." He elaborates, "The only possible silver lining to this cloud is that the owners and players will hurt themselves so badly that they will never be tempted to do this again."[147]

The disdain for the players was so great that some were even quick to exalt the memory of the former replacement players, who represented, by contrast, admirable vestiges of a

[145] "Letters: Bury the Hatchet," *Sports Illustrated* September 18, 1995.
[146] "Letters," *Sports Illustrated* August 29, 1994.
[147] Steve Wulf, "Fans, Strike Back!," *Sports Illustrated* September 26, 1994.

bygone era: "Collectively, they were willing participants in as distasteful a scheme as was ever foisted on the American sporting public," wrote *Buffalo News* reporter Gordon Edes. "Individually, they were the Everyman Ballplayer as we wish more major leaguers resembled – humble, good natured, and always willing to accommodate the fans. There's no place in the record books for replacement performances, but baseball could do worse than preserve for posterity the way the replacements conducted themselves."[148]

It was somewhat ironic that in September, 1994, Ken Burns's *Baseball* documentary premiered on television, reminding viewers of the halcyon days that stood in such sharp relief to the current climate surrounding the sport. The documentary "spoke dearly to those who love the game," wrote one reviewer, "but [who] feel little affection for

[148] Gordon Edes, "Field of Pipe Dreams Coming to End," *Buffalo News* April 2, 1995: B4.

today's owners, players and satellites (agents, the media) who make huge sums of money but crave ever more."[149]

The emotions articulated by these fans and countless others show how the strike did substantial harm to the relationship between fans and the entire institution of baseball. By 1994, greed on the part of the owners was already generally expected, but many for the first time voiced outrage at the same outward display of greed by the players. This indignation toward the players, even given that it was the owners who were forcing the issue, is especially telling. The resulting rift that formed between Major League Baseball and its fans would not be easily repaired.

[149] Robert McDowell, "When Baseball Made Out," *The Hudson Review* Vol. 48 No. 3 (Autumn 1995), 412.

The Next CBA & Luxury Tax

Negotiations for the next basic agreement began almost immediately after the strike ended. Neither side was quick to abandon their original pre-injunction position, but in light of the catastrophic experience of the last strike, both sides were equally averse to another work stoppage. By late October 1996, both sides agreed to a deal in principle made between the MLBPA and the owners' new lead negotiator, Randy Levine. A former labor commissioner of New York City, Levine had an easygoing approach and a personality that was inoffensive to all involved.[150] The agreement they drafted contained several modest reforms with few drastic, sweeping changes, with one exception: the introduction of a revenue sharing system.

---

[150] Zimbalist, *In the Best Interests of Baseball?,* 150.

The owners met to review the proposed CBA on November 6, 1996, voting 18-12 against the agreement. In a dumbfounding series of events, the proposal was at first voted down, as the owners were effectively persuaded once again by the same hostile voices among them that had hastened and sustained the strike. Chief among these antagonists was Chicago White Sox owner Jerry Reinsdorf, who adamantly opposed any settlement that did not include a salary cap. However, the owners' resolve was finally broken by the comically ill-advised actions of Reinsdorf himself. After urging his fellow owners to reject a settlement and preaching financial restraint, Reinsdorf only a few weeks later signed free agent Albert Belle to a 5-year, $55 million deal, the largest free-agent contract ever awarded at the time. "The small market teams should know I've always been with them. I've always been a leader in the push for revenue sharing," Reinsdorf told reporters. "Hey, I think the system stinks, but for now it's the system we're all operating under, and I've got to remain competitive."[151]

Reinsdorf's deceitful folly led to the dissolution of the opposition to settlement that he once spearheaded, and when the owners voted again on November 26, the agreement was almost unanimously approved.[152] *Sports Illustrated* writer Gerry Callahan put it particularly well: "To his peers, Reinsdorf would not have appeared more duplicitous if he had been caught in a hot tub with Fehr. At least we can thank Reinsdorf for one thing: There will be no talk of collusion."[153]

The most important facets of the 1996 CBA were the inclusion of a revenue sharing scheme with a corresponding luxury tax,

[151] Gerry Callahan, "Double Play," *Sports Illustrated* December 2, 1996.
[152] The second time around, Reinsdorf was one of only four votes against, along with especially small-market Oakland, Cleveland, and Kansas City teams. Remarkably, fourteen other owners were swayed to reverse their votes toward support of the new agreement.
[153] Gerry Callahan, "Double Play," *Sports Illustrated* December 2, 1996.

intended to allow teams to share more equally in the game's spoils. The sharing system, to be rolled out incrementally over the next five years, would tax each team at 20 percent of its net revenue. Three quarters of these funds would be distributed equally to all the clubs in a so-called "straight pool" system, with the remaining quarter used in a "split pool" system going directly to further supplement the clubs with below-average revenue. Additionally, the teams with the top five payrolls were charged with paying an additional 35% "luxury tax" on the amount by which they exceeded the luxury "threshold," or the midpoint between the fifth- and sixth- highest team payrolls.[154] These funds would then be distributed to the bottom thirteen teams by revenue. The luxury tax was designed as a substitute for a salary cap, but with the richest owners, rather than the players, bearing

[154] Zimbalist, *In the Best Interests of Baseball?*, 151.

the burden of any attempt to keep salaries down across the league.

Still, neither side was left overjoyed with the new arrangement. Owners felt that a lack of salary cap could prove an insufficient drag on rising salaries, while players felt a luxury tax would serve to discourage owners from signing big-money contracts. In that sense, it was a true compromise. "This is a landmark day for baseball," Bud Selig said upon ratification of the deal. "We can now work together to bring peace to the game and reconnect the sport to all of our fans."[155]

The 1996 agreement's additional provisions were relatively benign. Minimum salaries were increased from $109,000 to $150,000, and eventually $200,000 in 1999. Measures for salary arbitration and free agency remained intact. The players even managed to convince the owners to give them credit for the

155 Peter Schmuck, "Finally! Baseball at Peace," *Florida Times Union* (Jacksonville, FL) November 27, 1996: D1.

service time that was lost due to the strike. The new deal also introduced the creation of an Industry Growth Fund (IGF) to promote the game domestically and abroad. The IGF was funded and managed jointly by the players and owners and acted as a symbol of cooperation by the two sides going forward. Finally, both sides agreed to put in place a mechanism to prevent a future strike, eventually manifested in Congressional passage of the Curt Flood Act of 1998. The Flood Act, backed in part by Kentucky Representative and Baseball Hall of Fame pitcher Jim Bunning, served as a partial lifting of MLB's federal anti-trust exemption. In practice, the law amounted to an expansion of the union's ability to seek legal action against the league in the event of a labor dispute, whereas previously their only leverage was the threat of a strike.[156] Passage of the Flood Act left all of Major League Baseball's other antitrust exemptions intact,

[156] Zimbalist, *In the Best Interests of Baseball?*, 152.

including broadcast rights, marketing, licensing, the player draft, and the expansion, sale, and relocation of teams.157

Teams' finances were also bolstered in other ways. A new and improved television deal was signed for the 1996 season with NBC and Fox. Free from the dreadful terms of the 1993 agreement and the Baseball Network fiasco, teams were once again set to receive up-front revenue from national broadcasters. The $1.7 billion deal doubled the gross national television revenue received by each club from $5.5 million in 1994 to $11 million in 1996.158 Additionally, two new expansion franchises were sold, with teams in Arizona and Tampa Bay entering MLB in 1998, each paying a $130 million expansion fee and expanding the league to thirty teams.159 Along with expansion, both leagues were

---

157 "Congress Throws a Strike," *Cincinnati Post* October 10, 1998.
158 Tom Verducci, "Trimming the Fat in Baseball," *Sports Illustrated* December 4, 1995.
159 Staudohar, *Playing for Dollars*, 51.

realigned from two to three divisions each, with each division winner making the playoffs along with a fourth wild card entrant. The creation of an eight-team postseason, along with an additional round of playoff games to sell, was a financial boon. New stadiums were built in Seattle and Milwaukee, joining teams like Texas and Baltimore in lucrative, publicly financed stadium deals replete with pricey luxury boxes.[160] Finally, the 1997 season saw regular-season, non-exhibition interleague games played for the first time, both in an effort to renew fan interest and stimulate attendance, especially in small-market stadiums.

Results of the Strike

The 232 days of the strike saw the cancellation of as many as 948 potential games. When all was said and done, the owners

[160] Mark Belko, "Super Stadiums: Bait or Burden?," *Pittsburgh Post-Gazette* October 29, 1995: A1.

announced losses of close to $1 billion, including lost revenue from ticket sales and television contracts. Player losses were as high as $300 million. Veteran players received regular checks from the union strike fund, but they were, after all, being paid back their own money. Many younger players got little or nothing.[161]

Baseball's attendance decreased immediately after the strike, falling from an average of 31,612 fans per game in 1994 to 25,021 in 1995.[162] The overall attendance drop of approximately 20% in 1995 was due to a combination of both fan resentment and a shortened 144-game season. Clubs tried to lure fans back with mixed results. To help rehabilitate its image, Major League Baseball hired the advertising firm Goodby, Silverstein & Partners, resulting in the hastily produced "Welcome to the Show" advertising campaign. The series of ads celebrated ancillary aspects of

[161] Lowenfish, *The Imperfect Diamond*, 296.
[162] Zimbalist, *May the Best Team Win,* 93.

baseball such as hot-dog vendors, ballpark organists, and perpetually downtrodden Cubs fans, presumably to shift focus away from the then-resented players and teams themselves. The campaign, "designed to show the bridge between the game, the players, and the fans," according MLB's PR staff, was a failure. Dedicated baseball fans quickly saw through the ploy, while casual viewers (*potential fans*, in advertiser-speak) were left confused by the baseball-specific jargon and imagery.[163] Individual teams mounted their own promotional campaigns, including deeply discounted tickets, increased player appearances before and after games, and expansion of local community outreach programs.

Owners claimed the 1994 schism was predicated on a lack of competitive balance in

[163] Robyn F. Bolton, "A Study of the Implications of the 1994 Major League Baseball Players' Strike and an Analysis of the Marketing Strategies Used by Major League Baseball and Four Teams in Response to the Strike," BHOF Central Archives: MFF 84 (1998): 10-12.

the game, but ironically, the revenue sharing scheme implemented under the 1996 CBA actually contributed to *decreased* competitive balance between big-market teams and small-market teams. The low-revenue teams quickly found that by lowering payrolls – and accordingly, lowering the quality of their on-field product – they would receive greater payouts from the central revenue sharing fund, amounting to increased profitability in fielding an inferior team. Payroll disparities increased accordingly: the ratio of the top to bottom team payroll went from 4.85 in 1995-96 to 7.72 from 1997-2001.[164] This dynamic was confirmed by Commissioner Selig's so-called Blue Ribbon Panel, appointed to research the "chronic competitive imbalance" issue in advance of the 2002 negotiations, whose report admitted that "some low-revenue clubs, believing the amount of their proceeds from revenue sharing

[164] Zimbalist, *May the Best Team Win,* 50.

insufficient to enable them to become competitive, used these proceeds to become modestly profitable."165

Fan interest was renewed somewhat by a few high points in the 1995 season. Cal Ripken successfully broke Lou Gehrig's streak by playing in his 2,131st consecutive game on September 6th, an accomplishment commended with great esteem by fans throughout the country. Several teams such as the Seattle Mariners, Cleveland Indians, and Atlanta Braves had outstanding seasons, bringing baseball enthusiasm back to home cities long-starved for winners. Fans also began to take notice as sluggers like Baltimore's Brady Anderson and Oakland's Mark McGwire put on impressive power displays with 50-plus home-run seasons.

Despite these high points, the game's popularity continued to wane. Total attendance league-wide plummeted from 70.2 million in

165 Gould, *Bargaining with Baseball*, 124.

1995 to 50.0 million in 1994, followed by a barely improved 50.4 million in 1995. Attendance increased slightly in 1996 and 1997, reaching 60.0 million and 63.1 million, respectively. Finally, in 1998, baseball made its first return to pre-strike attendance totals, bringing in 70.3 million fans, as the summer of 1998 saw the home-run mania hinted at in the previous few seasons reach a boiling point.[166] McGwire, now with St. Louis, along with Chicago Cubs slugger Sammy Sosa, competed in a dramatic chase to break Roger Maris's 61-home run season, and America was fully enthralled. When Associated Press reporter Steve Wilstein discovered the anabolic steroid "andro" in McGwire's locker, a drug that was illegal on the street but not formally banned by Major League Baseball, it was the reporter, not the player, who received harsh criticism from all sides. Cardinals manager Tony LaRussa wanted to revoke

[166] Associated Press, "MLB Attendance Drops 1.2 Percent This Year," *USA Today* October 1, 2013.

Wilstein's media credentials, and his fellow reporters distanced themselves from their colleague. Players Association rep Gene Orza said that steroid use would not be discussed "at a time when McGwire's chase of the home run record might be compromised."[167] The superhuman displays of strength and power from McGwire and many others had quickly become baseball's main draw among average American sports fans. No one involved in baseball was willing to sabotage what seemed to be "saving" the game in the wake of the strike.

Of course, there are well-documented examples of steroid-fueled teams before 1994, such as Oakland's so-called "Bash Brothers" of the late 80's. Indeed, the use of performance-enhancing drugs, including steroids, amphetamines, and other substances, took place for decades prior to the strike, and to draw a direct cause-and-effect relationship between the

167 Lowenfish, *The Imperfect Diamond*, 300.

two is overly reductionist. Nevertheless, it is worthwhile to consider the proliferation of steroid use that exploded, virtually unchecked, in the strike's wake. "Obviously, the players who illegally used performance enhancing substances are responsible for their actions," wrote former Senator George Mitchell in his 2007 report on PED abuse in baseball. "But they did not act in a vacuum. Everyone involved in baseball over the past two decades – Commissioners, club officials, the Players Association, and players – shares to some extent in the responsibility for the steroids era."[168] In their mutually complicit acceptance of steroid use, owners and players created what may be the ultimate legacy of the 1994-95 strike by carelessly forfeiting whatever measure of baseball's purity or innocence that remained in exchange for a quick financial rebound.

---

[168] George J. Mitchell, "Report to the Commissioner of Baseball of an Independent Investigation into the Illegal Use of Steroids and Other Performance Enhancing Substances by Players in Major League Baseball," December 13 2007, SR-36.

Baseball continued to recover. Industry
revenues doubled in the period from 1996 to
2001, a fact made possible, no doubt, by the
ability of players and owners to avoid another
work stoppage. 169 In 2002, the 1996 CBA
expired and a new agreement was signed
without a corresponding strike or lockout,
marking the first time the two sides were able to
settle a contract amicably since 1972. The new
contract made improvements upon many of the
shortcomings of the prior agreement, including
increased drug testing and a modified revenue
sharing scheme to discourage small-market
teams from abusing the system. In turn, several
bottom-revenue teams showed that successful
seasons were possible on a budget, including
2002's 103-win Oakland Athletics immortalized
in Michael Lewis' *Moneyball*, along with the 2003
World Champion Florida Marlins and the 2008

169 Zimbalist, *May the Best Team Win*, 93.

AL Champion Tampa Bay Rays.[170] Other clubs show that abuses are still possible: in 2008, the Pittsburgh Pirates received about $75 million in shared revenue from Major League Baseball and only invested $48 million in payroll, netting a tidy $27 million profit before selling a single ticket. The team finished squarely in last place.[171]

Conclusion

The owners of Major League Baseball's 28 teams, incited and provoked by an aggressive cabal of small-market franchise holders, sought to drastically change the course along which the business of baseball had been heading since the advent of free agency in 1975. The 1994-95 strike was to be the final showdown that would finally break the players union and realign the economics of the game in their favor. Instead of a decisive victory, however, the result was an attritional, grinding standoff that saw the World Series cancelled for the first time in nearly a

[170] Gould, *Bargaining with Baseball*, 124.
[171] *Ibid.*, 130.

century. Writes *The New York Times'* Claire Smith, "Labor discord managed to do what the Kaiser, Hitler, and the Great Depression could not: to bring the national pastime to the ground in ignominious defeat and disgrace."[172]

If the strike produced any winners, it was certainly the Players Association. The owners, despite their best efforts, could not break the union. Many owners who were successful in breaking unions in their outside businesses expected the same triumphs in dealing with the players. In that sense, the baseball strike defied the larger trend of union busting in late 20th-century America. Despite becoming increasingly fractured, though, the owners never capitulated. Both sides were willing to go past the brink without compromise, apparently without regard for the collateral damage that was being done to the game. It took a bolt from the blue, in the

[172] Claire Smith, "Take 700 Players and 28 Owners and It Winds Up to 0 Solution," *New York Times* September 15, 1994: B13.

form of a federal court injunction, to turn back the clock and force an end to the standoff.

"Some say that Sotomayor saved baseball," quipped President Barack Obama, who would appoint the judge to the Supreme Court. Others disagree, like columnist George F. Will, who excoriates baseball's so-called savior: "What she did was take sides, took union's side against the management, and in so-doing, wasted 262 days of negotiations. That, far from saving baseball, consigned baseball to seven more years of an unreformed economic system, which happened to be the seven worst years in terms of competitive balance." Sotomayor's heavy-handedness merely "delayed the restructuring of baseball," Will says. "In fact, baseball thrives now because we got over the damage that her judicial activism did in that strike."[173] Whether baseball has gone on to prosper as a result of Sotomayor's actions or despite them, the fact

[173] "Did Sotomayor Save Baseball?" *The Economist* May 27, 2009.

remains that baseball has flourished economically since the strike. As *ESPN's* Peter Gammons put it, "She saved the owners from themselves. Sotomayor forced the game to resume and changed the way that they bargain in real faith, and baseball under Selig went from $1.3 billion to a $7.5 billion business."[174]

However, even if baseball has thrived economically, its success in the twenty-odd years since the strike ended has come at the price of irreversible damage to its soul. The perception of the greed of "millionaires against billionaires" driving the game is gone from the headlines, but remains, like a traumatic event from childhood, burned into baseball's collective subconscious. Indeed, just as each baseball fan in every generation experiences his or her own individual moment of lost innocence as childhood idealism collides with adult realities, so too does the

[174] Allen Barra, "Baseball's Costliest Walk," *Wall Street Journal* October 28, 2009.

strike represent that same pivotal moment in the maturation of baseball itself. Author Karl Wenclas, writing while the strike was still underway, encapsulated the sentiment of many baseball fans particularly well, articulating a feeling that is both jaded and optimistic at once: "I know that when the baseball strike is over I'll be back attending the games, one with the mob. The strike is like a force of nature you can do nothing about. If you love the game you love it with all its faults – silly scoreboards, crazy mascots, greedy players and owners among them."[175] The 1994-95 strike was the anvil on which contemporary baseball was shaped. It was the point at which modern baseball became *post-modern* baseball, as baseball fandom, among all but the most naïve, is now permanently imbued with an underlying cynicism and distrust.

[175] Karl Wenclas, "American Eye: The Last Day of Baseball," *The North American Review* Vol. 279 No. 6 (Nov. – Dec. 1994): 11.

Bibliography

Anderson, Sparky with Dan Ewald. *They Call Me Sparky.* Chelsea, MI: Sleeping Bear Press, 1998.

Babson, Steve. *The Unfinished Struggle: Turning Points in American Labor, 1877-Present.* Lanham, MD: Rowman & Littlefield, 1999.

Barth, Gunther. *City People: The Rise of Modern City Culture in Nineteenth-Century America.* Oxford and New York: Oxford University Press, 1980.

Bolton, Robyn F. "A Study of the Implications of the 1994 Major League Baseball Players' Strike and an Analysis of the Marketing Strategies Used by Major League Baseball and Four Teams in Response to the Strike." BHOF Central Archives: MFF 84, 1998.

Cohen, Russ with Nikco Riesgo. *Strike Three: A Player's Journey through the Infamous Baseball Strike of 1994.* Raleigh, HC: Lulu.com, 2009.

Corcoran, Kieran M. "When Does the Buzzer Sound?: The Nonstatutory Labor

Exemption in Professional Sports."
Columbia Law Review Vol. 94, No. 3 (April
1994): 1045-1075.

Flynn, Neil F. *Baseball's Reserve System: The Case
and Trial of Curt Flood v. Major
League Baseball.* Springfield, IL: Walnut
Park Group, 2006.

Gould IV, William B. *Bargaining with Baseball:
Labor Relations in an Age of
Prosperous Turmoil.* Jefferson, NC:
McFarland & Co., 2011.

Gould IV, William B. "Baseball and Globalization:
The Game Played and Heard and
Watched 'Round the World (With
Apologies to Soccer and Bobby
Thomson)." *Indiana Journal of Global
Legal Studies,* Vol. 8, No. 1 (Fall 2000): 85-
120.

Heylar, John. *Lords of the Realm: The Real History
of Baseball.* New York: Ballantine,
1994.

Leyden, Joe. *The Great American Baseball Strike.*
Brookfield, CT: Millbrook Press,
1995.

Lichtenstein, Nelson. *State of the Union: A
Century of American Labor.* Princeton:
Princeton University Press, 2003.

Lieberman Research Inc. "How Baseball Fans Feel About A Possible Strike," Bowie K Kuhn Collection: BA MSS 100, National Baseball Hall of Fame & Museum (Cooperstown, NY): March, 1980.

Lowe, John. "The Passing of a Legend." *Sparky Anderson: The Life of a Baseball Legend.* Edited by Tom Panzenhagen and Barry Forbis. Chicago: Triumph Books, 2010.

Lowenfish, Lee. *The Imperfect Diamond: A History of Baseball's Labor Wars.* Lincoln, NE: University of Nebraska Press, 2010.

McCartin, Joseph A. *Collision Course: Ronald Reagan, The Air Traffic Controllers, and the Strike that Changed America.* New York: Oxford University Press, 2011.

McDowell, Robert. "When Baseball Made Out." *The Hudson Review* Vol. 48 No. 3 (Autumn 1995): 411-424.

Miller, Marvin. *A Whole Different Ball Game: The Inside Story of the Baseball Revolution.* Chicago: Ivan R. Dee, 1991, 2004.

Mitchell, George J. "Report to the Commissioner of Baseball of an Independent Investigation

Into the Illegal Use of Steroids and Other
Performance Enhancing Substances by
Players in Major League Baseball."
December 13 2007.
http://files.mlb.com/mitchrpt.pdf

Morris, Peter. *A Game of Inches: The Story Behind
the Innovations that Shaped
Baseball.* Chicago: Ivan R. Dee, 2010.

Noll, Roger G. "Baseball Economics in the 1990s:
A Report to the Major League
Baseball Players Association (Public
Version)." BHOF Central Archives: MFF3,
National Baseball Hall of Fame & Museum
(Cooperstown, NY): 1994.

Schwarz, Alan. "'94 in Review." *Baseball America
1995 Almanac.* Edited by Allan Simpson.
Durham, NC: Baseball America, 1995.

Schwarz, Alan. "'95 in Review." *Baseball America
1996 Almanac.* Edited by Allan Simpson.
Durham, NC: Baseball America, 1996.

Staudohar, Paul D. *Playing for Dollars: Labor
Relations and the Sports Business.*
Ithaca and London: Cornell University
Press, 1996.

Staudohar, Paul D. "The Baseball Strike of 1994-
95." *Monthly Labor Review* March
1997: 21-27.

Staudohar, Paul D. "Baseball's Changing Salary Structure." *Compensation and Working Conditions* Fall 1997: 2-9.

Wenclas, Karl. "American Eye: The Last Day of Baseball." *The North American Review* Vol. 279 No. 6 (Nov. – Dec. 1994): 4-11.

Zimbalist, Andrew. *In the Best Interests of Baseball?: The Revolutionary Reign of Bud Selig*. Hoboken: John Wiley & Sons, 2006.

Zimbalist, Andrew. *May the Best Team Win: Baseball Economics and Public Policy*. Washington, DC: Brookings Institution Press, 2003.

Periodicals

Chapter 1

"Substitute Detroit Game." *New York Times* May 9, 1912.

Harper, Paul. "He Started It All: Ward Led 1890 Revolt." *Boston Globe* June 21, 1981.

Kaplan, Jim. "No Games Today." *Sports Illustrated* June 22, 1981: 17-21.

Chapter 2

Associated Press. "Baseball Owners Claim Union
Threatening Replacement Players." *The
Ottawa Citizen* (Ottawa, ON) January 19,
1995: D8.

Associated Press, "More Baseball Fans Vowing to
Skip Replacement Games," *Salt Lake
Tribune* March 27, 1995: C2.

Bevans, Michael. "Let's Make a Deal." *Sports
Illustrated* February 20, 1995.

Blair, Jeff. "A Last Hurrah for Walker; Baseball
Strike Might End His Career with
Expos." *The Gazette* (Montreal, QC)
August 04, 1994: D1.

Blum, Ronald. "Baseball Seeks Job Applicants."
York Daily Record (York, PA) January 14,
1995.

Bodley, Hal. "Lineup Crowded for Today's
Baseball Talks." *USA Today* August 24,
1994: 01A.

Chass, Murray. "Owners Unveil Salary Cap to a
Chilly Reception from Players."
New York Times June 15, 1994: B.13.

Chass, Murray. "Baseball: Under Proposal,
Players Could Get Lesser Share." *New*

York Times June 18, 1994: 1.31.

Chass, Murray. "Brushback Pitch: Owners to Kill Pension Payment." *New York Times* August 3, 1994: B.7.

Chass, Murray. "Hatch Hopeful on Antitrust Repeal." *New York Times* February 14, 1995: B.10.

Cooper, Barry. "Advertisers Aren't Buying Replacement Baseball." *Oakland Post* (Oakland, CA) March 8, 1995: 11.

Dailey, Ken. "Skipper is Chiper: Lasorda Misses Players but Has Rapt Audience." *Daily News* (Los Angeles) March 21, 1995: S1.

DiGiovanna, Mike. "Langston Has Harsh Words for Fill-Ins." *Los Angeles Times* March 7, 1995.

Holtzman, Jerome. "Owners Reopen Basic Agreement, but Lockout Unlikely in '93." *Chicago Tribune* December 8, 1992.

Justice, Richard. "Players Object to Salary Cap; No Strike Date Set; Next Meeting is July." *Washington Post* June 17, 1994: D07.

Klis, Mike. "McMorris Gloomy After Talks Fail, Meeting with Fehr Fails to Open

Discussion." *Colorado Springs Gazette-Telegraph* September 3, 1995: C5.

Kurkjian, Tim. "Throwing Curves." *Sports Illustrated* January 09, 1994.

Litke, Jim. "Union Cautions Minor Leaguers, Players Warn Spring 'Scabs'." *The Commercial Appeal* (Memphis, TN) February 23, 1995: D.2.

Maske, Mark. "No Talks as Hopes Keep Fading." *Washington Post* September 2, 1994: F06.

Maske, Mark. "'Oil' and 'Air' Are an Odd Mix in Spring Camp." *Washington Post* February 19, 1995: D.01.

Maske, Mark. "At the Ol' (Replacement) Ball Game." *Washington Post* March 26, 2995: A1.

McCallum, Jack. "Blame the Bosses." *Sports Illustrated* October 10, 1994.

Miller, Jeff. "A Winning Day for Replacement Fan," *Orange County Register* (Santa Ana, CA) March 2, 1995: A01.

Neikirk, William. "His Baseball Jawboning Fails, So Clinton Turns to Congress." *Chicago Tribune* February 08, 1997.

Newhan, Ross. "Players Might Move Up Strike Date." *Los Angeles Times* August 4, 1994: D.1

Newhan, Ross. "Ravitch Derided by Fehr." *Los Angeles Times* August 23, 1994: 1.

Newhan, Ross. "Baseball Season, Series Cancelled: Owners Say Failure to Reach Bargaining Accord and 34-Day Players' Strike Made it Impossible to Resume Play." *Los Angeles Times* September 15, 1994: 1.

Newhan, Ross. "Players Draw the Line Against Replacement Games, Records." *Los Angeles Times March* 16, 1995: 3.

Stark, Jayson. "Minor Leaguers Facing Major Quandary." *Philadelphia Inquirer* February 20, 1995: C.1.

Stone, Larry. "Giants Don Kid Gloves to Handle 2 Camps in 1." *San Francisco Examiner* February 16, 1995: D.1.

Telander, Rick. "A Minor Adjustment." *Sports Illustrated* November 21, 1994.

VanDyck, Dave. "Sides Headed Back to Table, Owners Indicate Salary Cap

Negotiable." *Chicago Sun-Times* August 24, 1994: 96.

Whitesdale, Larry. "Bottom Line: No Settlement, So No Games," *Boston Globe* August 12, 1994: 37.

Chapter 3

Associated Press, "Balls & Strikes Replace Strike, Opener Lets Baseball Fans Forgive," *Salt Lake Tribune*, April 26, 1995: B.1.

Associated Press, "MLB Attendance Drops 1.2 Percent This Year," *USA Today* October 1, \ 2013.

Barra, Allen. "Baseball's Costliest Walk." *Wall Street Journal* October 28, 2009.

Belko, Mark. "Super Stadiums: Bait or Burden?" *Pittsburgh Post-Gazette* October 29, 1995: A1.

Blum, Ronald. "Fehr Has New Offer for Teams." *Pittsburgh Post-Gazette* March 30, 1995: D1.

Callahan, Gerry. "Double Play." *Sports Illustrated* December 2, 1996.

"Congress Throws a Strike," *Cincinnati Post* October 10, 1998.

Cowan, Stu. "There Just Weren't Enough 'Real' Baseball Fans Here." *The Gazette* (Montreal, QC) April 24, 2005: C5.

Delcos, John. "Baseball Enters Home Stretch." *York Daily Record* (York, PA) April 3, 1995: 01.

"Did Sotomayor Save Baseball?" *The Economist* May 27, 2009.

Edes, Gordon. "Field of Pipe Dreams Coming to End." *Buffalo News* April 2, 1995: B4.

Hummell, Rick. "Baseball Lockout Unlikely: Owners Postpone Season Opener, Send Replacement Players Packing." *St. Louis Post-Dispatch* April 2, 1995: 01.A.

Kurkjian, Tim. "Baseball: Expo Economics." *Sports Illustrated* August 8, 1994.

Kurkjian, Tim. "Star Bursts." *Sports Illustrated* September 26, 1994.

"Letters." *Sports Illustrated* August 29, 1994.

"Letters: Bury the Hatchet." *Sports Illustrated* September 18, 1995.

Maske, Mark. "Baseball Players Offer to End Strike; Federal Judge Rules Against Owners." *Washington Post* April 01, 1995: A.01.

Newhan, Ross. "Baseball Players Offer to End
232-Day Strike." *Los Angeles Times* April 1,
1995: 1.

Schmuck, Peter. "Finally! Baseball at Peace."
Florida Times Union (Jacksonville, FL)
November 27, 1996: D1.

Smith, Claire. "Take 700 Players and 28 Owners
and It Winds Up to 0 Solution." *New
York Times* September 15, 1994: B13.

Stark, Jayson. "Finally, Baseball Opens '95
Season." *Philadelphia Inquirer* April 26, 1995:
D.1.

Swift, E.M. and Richard O'Brien. "They Said It."
Sports Illustrated August 22, 1994.

Thomas, Robert McG, Jr. "Baseball: If It's Over,
'94 Season Had Tight Races and Individual
Accomplishments." *New York Times*
August 12, 1994: B11.

Thomas, Robert McG Jr. "Baseball: The Fans;
Booooooo! Crowd Doesn't Like Call." *New
York Times* September 15, 1994: B12.

Verducci, Tom. "Trimming the Fat in Baseball."
Sports Illustrated December 4, 1995.

Wulf, Steve. "Fans, Strike Back!" *Sports Illustrated* September 26, 1994.